— PRAISE FOR —
Libertarianism In One Lesson

"The best brief introdu[...] Bergland is anxious to provi[...] [compreh]ensive a case as he can, and waste [...]g to the point... He has even adapted it so it c[...] readily used in classrooms, and [includes questions] differentiating among liberal, conservative, and libertarian positions on current issues."
— Radio talk show host **Brian Wilson**

"Thought-provoking reading."
— **Students for Self-Government at Chico State University**

"Many authors try to write the last word on a subject. David Bergland has done something far harder. He has written the *first* word on libertarianism. *Libertarianism in One Lesson* is a brief and bright introduction to the core ideas, principles, and applications of libertarianism."
— **Michael Cloud**, author of *Secrets of Libertarian Persuasion*

"Explain[s] libertarianism as a coherent, principled philosophy with strong implications for public policy..."
— **Jim Strawhorn**, *LPQC News*

"Clearly shows the fundamental differences among the liberal, conservative, and libertarian ethical views."
— **David King**, RKBA.org

"A primer for those who are new to the libertarian movement."
— **UndercoverBooks.com**

"I was cleaning off my desk, and I came across some papers... Amongst them was David Bergland's *Libertarianism In One Lesson*. I decided to read a little of it to decide whether to throw it [out] or keep it. I did not put it down until I had finished."
— **Neal Randall**, Vermont State Representative (1998-2000)

"[Explains] what libertarianism is and its application to society."
— **FreedomLibrary.com**

"Excellent." — *Liberty News* (Boulder County, Colorado)

Libertarianism In One Lesson

NINTH EDITION

Libertarianism In One Lesson

NINTH EDITION

By David Bergland

THE ADVOCATES FOR SELF-GOVERNMENT

Published October 2005. FIRST PRINTING.

Bergland, David
Libertarianism In One Lesson, Ninth Edition
By David Bergland
ISBN 0-9754326-4-8
1. Libertarianism   2. Political philosophy   3. Politics
I. Title   II. Bergland, David

Manufactured in the United States of America
Typography and Cover Design by Bill Winter

This Ninth Edition of Libertarianism In One Lesson
comes into the world 21 years after the First Edition.
My wife, Sharon Ayres, and I have been married the same 21 years.
With her unwavering love and support, I have been able to
write when and how I wanted and to live the same way.
This book is dedicated to Sharon Ayres, in every way
the best human being I have ever known.

ACKNOWLEDGMENTS

After the Eighth Edition of this book was published in 2000, I decided that was enough. Apparently, I was wrong. Last year, Sharon Harris, president of the Advocates for Self-Government, made me an offer I could not refuse. The Advocates would publish a Ninth Edition of the book and I would have the assistance of the talented writers Bill Winter and Jimmy Harris to do research, writing, and editing to bring the Ninth Edition of the book up to date. So, what you see is a collaborative effort, and I am very pleased with the result. Most assuredly, I would not and could not have finished the book as it is without Bill and Jimmy. The page layout and cover design are the work of Bill Winter. I also want to thank Evelyn Hanson who did the final proofreading. Sharon Harris has overseen the entire effort, from the opening suggestion, through cracking the whip with her usual finesse and effectiveness, to the end product you have in your hands. Without her, this book would not exist. As the author, I take full responsibility for the contents, good, bad, so-so, right, wrong, odd, or whatever else the case may be.

David Bergland
September 2005

TABLE OF CONTENTS

PREFACE TO THE NINTH EDITION

I wrote the first edition of *Libertarianism In One Lesson* during my 1984 Libertarian presidential campaign. I designed it as a first look into that uniquely American philosophy of freedom — libertarianism. As I had hoped, its appeal and usefulness have continued well beyond the 1984 election.

In 1988, an underground publisher in Poland requested permission to translate the book into Polish and publish it there. I happily gave permission. The publication of such a radically pro-freedom book in communist Poland was quite risky for those brave underground publishers. In spite of that, the project was a success and the book was distributed in Poland. It amuses and delights me to think that it may have played some role in the revolutionary events of 1989.

During 1989 and 1990, communist governments and socialist economies collapsed everywhere. Privatization, free-market reforms, and democratic political reform swept the world. The Fifth Edition, published in 1990, the Sixth Edition in 1993, the Seventh Edition in 1997, and the Eighth Edition in 2000 were each modified to reflect these new events.

The Seventh Edition also added chapters on the health-care crisis and the crucial issue of the right to keep and bear arms (including its relationship to crime and personal security). The Eighth Edition added a final chapter entitled "Toward a Constitutional Federal Government," arguing for a federal government limited to only those powers and functions expressly granted in the Constitution.

This new Ninth Edition represents another milestone for the book. It has been extensively updated and revised. Additional facts, quotations, and source citations have been added in an effort to make the book more useful. The Advocates for Self-Government, one of the libertarian movement's leading educational organizations, has stepped forward as publisher. More than 20 years after its first edition, I am confident that the book is more relevant and timely than ever.

The Soviet Union and the Cold War are no more. Former Soviet republics are now independent. After 70 years of Soviet totalitarianism, progress toward the free market is understandably slow, and many old Communist Party apparatchiks oppose change. But change is inevitable, in light of the informational freedom that now exists in the former communist world, and the irrepressible hunger of people for personal freedom. In many countries, democratic elections have installed popular governments, ending decades of despotism. It is gratifying that many of these changes have taken directions advocated in earlier editions of this book.

All of the news is not good. In the United States, the insane "War on Drugs" has intensified, and our civil liberties suffer from it. Since the terrorist attack of September 11, 2001, our civil liberties have declined further under the PATRIOT Act. Too many politicians and the media continue to indulge the delusion that the president and Congress can, by intrusive action, "fix" the economy. Democratic and Republican politicians continue to act as if every stress and strain in our lives is a proper subject for their attention, while they blind themselves to the evidence that everything they touch gets worse. They also believe that America's foreign policy role should be that of international policeman and nanny, a view on the increase since 9/11. As a result, our nation is embroiled in another bloody foreign war.

To the reader new to libertarianism, this book provides some fundamental principles and their application to current issues. Libertarianism is dynamic and evolving, as anything in the marketplace of ideas must be. My hope is that you will question every concept presented here, and every idea you have learned about political economy elsewhere, and thus be stimulated to investigate further. If this book becomes your first step on a journey to greater political awareness, then I feel I have done my job as an author.

Because I am a libertarian, my confident view is that the more free and open inquiry we have into these issues, the closer we will come to that most desirable state of affairs in which both you and I will be respected and appreciated as the unique and competent individuals we are.

David Bergland
Kennewick, Washington
September 2005

INTRODUCTION

A book with the title *Libertarianism In One Lesson* might be expected to contain one lesson, one central idea or theme, to help explain all that is discussed in the book. Here it is:

YOU OWN YOURSELF.

The statement "you own yourself" may not seem so remarkable. If you believe no one should kill you, enslave you, beat you, or steal from you, then you probably feel fairly comfortable with the "self-ownership" principle. But, what does it mean to "own" something?

To own something means that *you decide* what to do with it. You can use it up, sell it, or keep it. Other people may not force you to do anything you don't want to do with what you own. To own yourself means that *your* decisions about what to do with your life, your body, your energy, speech, action, and honestly acquired property are the decisions that count. No one has the right to force you to act against your own interests as you see them.

But since people are equal, not only do you own yourself, every *other* person owns himself or herself. So each of us must respect the right of each other person to run his or her own life. You cannot force other people to act as you wish. You have no right to kill them, enslave them, beat them, or steal from them, no matter how much good you think it might do. Consequently, you must take responsibility for yourself. Even your most urgent desires, interests, or alleged "needs" do not constitute a valid moral claim on the life, earnings, or property of another person.

The self-ownership principle draws a line around each individual, creating a zone of privacy and freedom of action. We must respect every other person's right to act within his or her zone. Yes, it may sometimes be difficult to determine exactly where my actions cross the line defining your zone. That's why we have courts of law to resolve disputes.

The important thing is that we agree on the self-ownership principle as our guide to action in dealing with others. It means, simply, respecting other people as equal to ourselves in moral stature and human dignity. It means everyone has the right to make all the decisions about his or her own life, body, action, speech, and honestly acquired property. It means each of us must take responsibility for our own actions, accepting and bearing the consequences of our decisions.

Libertarians approach political, economic, and social issues by placing the highest priority on letting people solve their own problems, their own way, according to *their own* values. This usually results in proposals to replace clumsy, counterproductive government approaches with more effective and compassionate *voluntary* cooperation. In this book, I will discuss how this nation would *improve* if we demanded that those in government accord each of us the respect we deserve as unique and competent individuals.

This book is primarily designed for people who want to learn more about libertarianism and the promise it holds for a better tomorrow. However, this book also offers students and teachers an introduction to the political philosophy of libertarianism. This book can assist a U.S. Government or Political Science instructor who desires to supplement course materials with accurate, up-to-date information about an important political movement, the philosophy on which it is based, its history, and its application to real-world issues.

For advanced students of political science, additional research will be required to deal comprehensively with the issues discussed here. Fortunately, there is a wealth of relevant scholarship available. (See the *Suggested Reading* chapter at the end of this book for a start.)

For a concerned American who desires only enough information to make intelligent decisions about one of today's most exciting and fastest-growing political alternatives, the material included here should provide a sound beginning.

CHAPTER ONE

THE NATURE OF GOVERNMENT

Government is that great fictitious entity by which everyone tries to live at the expense of everyone else. — Frederic Bastiat

Government is not an entity or thing that exists independently of the people who make it up. Many different people in our society are part of "government." They include the president, senators, governors, judges, members of Congress, state legislators, city council members, police officers, jailers, building and fire inspectors, librarians, rubbish collectors, teachers, and so on. Every one of them is an ordinary person, just like you and me. They are nothing special.

And there is, in reality, no real, concrete entity called "government." There are millions of individuals, doing things we call "governmental functions," but that is all.

RULES OF CONDUCT, CRIMINAL PENALTIES, ARREST AND PROSECUTION

The critical feature of government action is that it works through force, coercion, and compulsion. Here is the pattern. Some ordinary people, called legislators, make rules of conduct and attach penalties for violation of the rules. When someone allegedly breaks a rule, they send people with guns (police officers) out to round up the accused and impose the penalty. This explanation may sound a bit simplistic, but it is not.

For example, Congress has established the rule that young men must register for the military draft. Any youth who fails to register is subject to criminal penalties. He will be arrested, charged, tried, and sent to jail if convicted.

Congress passes tax laws requiring Americans to deliver part of their incomes to the government's collection agency, the Internal Revenue Service. Failure to comply results in criminal prosecution. The IRS can seize the property of citizens who, it claims, have not paid taxes. If the citizen resists, his resistance is also a crime, ultimately leading to jail.

Congress has passed laws making it a crime to possess, buy, or sell certain natural substances — marijuana, for instance. Congress has also made it a crime to own certain types of weapons. Anyone found in possession of such contraband will be arrested by the government enforcers, charged, tried, and fined or sent to jail if convicted.

On the local level, city councils pass rules telling people what businesses they can conduct, what kind of buildings they must have for their businesses, and where they can locate them. Any violation of these rules will result in enforcers with guns going out to issue citations, make arrests, and proceed with criminal prosecution against the violators.

The ordinary people in government who make the rules and regulations for the rest of us are not very imaginative. Lawmaking is always the same. The legislature (whether city council, county supervisors, state legislature, or Congress) decides that something is a "problem." So they establish rules of conduct which will supposedly solve the problem, devise a criminal penalty for failure to comply, and establish a procedure for police and prosecutors to impose the penalty by force.

Some government programs might not appear to fit this pattern, such as Social Security, national defense, the Postal Service, or public schools. In those cases, politicians are responding to a perceived "need" from the people who elect and re-elect them to office. But the method of financing government programs — whether that program will allegedly solve a problem or address a need — remains the same. It is coercive taxation. Tax collectors compel citizens to deliver portions of their earnings (or other property) to pay for these government programs. Anyone who doesn't pay the tax runs the risk of going to jail.

People frequently say, "There ought to be a law," or "The government ought to take action." What they are *really* saying is that legislators should make certain rules, attach penalties to them, and send out men with guns to enforce those rules. They are also saying that people who disagree with their proposed rules should be punished — by fines, jail time, or death — if they violate them. People rarely talk about laws in such grim, stark terms. But behind every law lies the threat of force. That's what makes it a law.

SOCIAL CONTRACT OR PROTECTION RACKET?

You've probably heard it said that we are all party to a "social contract." That is, people claim there is a "social contract" that binds all the citizens of a country together. Usually this is part of an argument that people must submit to government controls and pay taxes as the price for living in an orderly society. But a binding contract requires persons to *voluntarily* enter an agreement, accepting obligations in exchange for benefits they expect to receive. An essential characteristic of a contract is that one can choose to enter it or not.

The history of the development of the state (government) shows that the state arose from conquest. One tribe or group would conquer another and exact tribute (taxes) in exchange for letting the conquered people live. The ruling tribe then protected the conquered tribe against other marauders. Rather than a "social contract," the relationship is more accurately described as a "protection racket."

Even in America — a nation born in a revolution against British arbitrary taxation and tyranny — the relationship between American citizens and the government is still not a social contract.

After all, how many people do you know who voluntarily signed the United States Constitution? How many have agreed to abide by the constitution of their home state? How many have *read* — much less given explicit approval to — the county charter, or city charter, where they reside? How many have any knowledge whatsoever of what these documents say?

The reality is: *There is no such thing as a social contract.* It is a pernicious myth. We must identify government for what it is: a group of ordinary people who have substantial, even lethal, power at their disposal. Further, they can, and do, use that power to control the rest of us.

The ultimate questions are: What is the legitimate use of government power? What standards should be used to determine whether those in government are using their power legitimately?

To answer these important questions, let us begin by looking at the actions of individual persons and the moral principles involved.

SELF-OWNERSHIP AND SELF-DEFENSE

Most people agree that it is proper for a person to use reasonable force in self-defense against an attacker. This is justified by the libertarian principle of self-ownership. Each individual owns himself or herself. No human owns another. To "own" something means you have the right to decide what to do with it, and, equally importantly, other people do not. As self-owners, each of us has the right to control our own lives, bodies, and property acquired by honest means. Each of us must also respect the equal rights of others. It follows that a person whose life, body, or property is threatened by another is within his rights to defend them with all necessary force.

If I have the right to defend myself, then it is also proper for other people to help me defend my rights, if necessary. This provides the answer to the question: "What is the legitimate use of government force?"

The people in government should be considered agents of the citizens. Government should be limited to helping the citizens defend their rights against any person or group who violates or threatens them.

Therefore, laws that penalize such actions as murder, rape, robbery, theft, embezzlement, fraud, arson, kidnapping, battery, trespass, or pollution (a form of trespass), are valid uses of government force. In each of those crimes, the perpetrators violate the rights of their victims.

By contrast, any activity that is peaceful, voluntary, and honest should be free from criminal penalties or government interference. There should be no laws, for instance, that penalize people for offering goods and services to willing consumers in the marketplace, for declining to be in the military, or for possessing things that others find objectionable.

GOVERNMENT MUST RESPECT RIGHTS

Many mistakenly assume that when a person becomes a government employee, he or she becomes an extraordinary person, acquiring special rights denied to others. But *there are no superior nor inferior human beings where rights are concerned.* The people in government have the same rights as the citizens. No more and no less. They also have the same obligation to respect the equal rights of others.

It is my right to defend myself. It is my right to authorize my agent, a public servant in government, to help me defend my rights. But I have no authority to violate the rights of others. Therefore, I cannot authorize the person in government to do so either. I cannot delegate a right I do not have.

You and I together, or a thousand of us, or a million of us, cannot morally violate the rights of another human — nor can our gang authorize the government to do so. Wrong does not become right just because the wrongdoers outnumber the victims, or because the wrong comes with a government stamp of approval.

Just as you and I must respect the rights of others, the people in government must carry out their legitimate functions in a way that respects the rights of the citizens — and does not violate them.

The essence of government is that government employees have force at their disposal. When is the use of that force legitimate? The answer is clear. Government power must be used *only* to protect the citizens from those who would violate their rights. The presumption should always be *against* the use of force. The burden to justify it should always be upon those who call for government action.

We must never fail to remember that when we call for government to act, we are asking the people in government to send out men with guns to control our fellow citizens, to take part of their earnings and property in taxes, to enforce rules of conduct against them, and to impose penalties if they fail to comply with the rules.

Even legitimate use of government force is dangerous. We must never call for its exercise unless it is clearly necessary to defend our rights or the rights of our fellow citizens.

CHAPTER TWO

THE ALTERNATIVE TO COERCIVE GOVERNMENT

There are two, and *only* two, ways for people to deal with each other. One way is by force. The other is by voluntary cooperation.

Government, at every level and in all its actions, is grounded in force. Here in the United States, from its creation until the middle of the nineteenth century, we had one particularly obvious and horrible institution based on force: slavery. Government power backed this abominable institution with the "fugitive slave" clause of the U.S. Constitution and the Fugitive Slave Acts passed by Congress.

It is clear that government, in all it does, is based on force. Just observe that if you refuse to obey a government regulation, you face fines, jail time, or death. Observe that government produces very little (and what it does produce is usually protected by monopolistic laws). And observe that people who work for the government receive their pay from other citizens through the coercive financing method called taxation.

Further, in almost all cases, you cannot choose to decline government services, operations, or activities and shop elsewhere. Taxpayers must pay for and submit to government action even when they disagree with it.

GOVERNMENT: A SERVICE CONGLOMERATE?

One way to view government is as a huge conglomerate of "service" businesses. Government employees provide many different services to the citizens, often in competition with private companies and individuals. For example, the Postal Service, power plants, schools, and trash disposal all compete with private alternatives. Even many services widely considered to be the purview of government have privately owned alternatives. For example, the courts (private mediation services), roads (private toll roads), the police (security guards), and prisons (privately operated jails).

Libertarians raise the following questions: (1) Must so-called "government services" be provided by government employees? (2) Must these services be paid for through coercion, by taxation? The answer to both questions is: No, not necessarily.

VOLUNTARY COOPERATION

Voluntary cooperation is the alternative to coercion as the basis for relationships among people. In our society we see many examples of voluntary cooperation in institutionalized form. The largest and most widespread is commercial activity — the marketplace. People, both as individuals and organized into companies, produce, buy, and sell millions of different products and services. In the free market, no one is forced to buy any particular product, nor from any particular seller. No one is forced to go into any particular line of work, nor to provide services or goods to any particular customer.

In a free-market transaction, each person enters it because, in his or her own judgment, the result will be beneficial. This is the key to understanding how free trade promotes economic development and increases productivity. When a participant enters into a transaction voluntarily, he expects to be better off according to his own values and priorities.

Contrast this with the transfer of property made under compulsion, when a person is forced to give up something at the point of a gun. Such a person will most likely *not* think he is better off. (After all, if he thought he would be better off, there would have been no need to *force* him to participate.)

RESPECT FOR RIGHTS

When the legal/political framework in a society respects and protects the rights of the people, then all can trade freely in the marketplace. In such circumstances, there would be no government intervention except when some people violated the rights of others by engaging in theft or fraud. The basis for productive trade relationships is respect for the rights of other people, and the conduct of trade on a peaceful, voluntary, and honest basis.

Many other institutions in our society are based on voluntary cooperation, such as churches and temples, the family, charitable institutions, medical research efforts, civic betterment organizations, and private schools. There are hundreds of thousands of groups and associations which Americans voluntarily join to accomplish goals of their own choosing. These organizations work remarkably well — particularly when compared to the typical bureaucratic bungling of government.

Underlying all this voluntary cooperation is the libertarian principle of respect for the rights of all people. Most people, most of the time, operate on the libertarian principle of respect for the rights of others. Most people do not want to control others and do not want others to control them. As private citizens, we almost always are peaceful and honest in our dealings with each other. We expect voluntary cooperation from our fellow citizens, and we usually get it.

PRIVATE PROPERTY: SELF OWNERSHIP

The legal foundation for this libertarian approach is the system of private property rights developed in English and American law. The most fundamental element is the concept of self-ownership; that is, each person owns himself or herself. No one owns other human beings.

When we speak of property, we usually think of land, buildings, or tangible personal property, such as automobiles, computers, money, surfboards, or whatever. In simplest terms, any person can acquire property beyond his or her own body by working to produce it, by trading peacefully and honestly with other owners of property, or by receiving gifts.

A legal system that protects the right of citizens to produce, acquire, and exchange property rights is an essential requirement for peaceful and productive relationships among people. The more clearly defined private property rights are, and the more dependable the legal protection for property rights, the easier it is for people to cooperate, and the better people are able to plan for their own futures. Dependable and secure property rights mean fewer disputes will arise over who can do what with any given piece of property.

WHO DECIDES?

Distinguishing between relationships based on force and those based on voluntary cooperation is extremely important. The crucial question is: *Who should decide what you can do with your life, with your body, and with your property?*

Libertarians answer that every person has the right to make *all* the decisions about his or her own life, body, and honestly acquired property. Further, each person must take responsibility for the consequences of his or her own decisions, good or bad. I have no right to force others to pay for my mistakes. I have no right to force others to bail out my business when my decisions lead to losses rather than profits. On the other hand, if your decisions provide you with positive benefits, these benefits are yours to keep or dispose of according to your values. Just as you must respect my rights, I must respect yours.

Voluntary cooperation is never a threat to a person's right to control his or her own life, body, and property. It is only the coercive mechanism of government (or the activities of habitual criminals) which constitute a threat to the rights of citizens.

Therefore, a major goal should be to confine government to its legitimate function of assisting the people in defending their rights against attacks or threats. Only when government is so limited will people have the maximum opportunity to develop the most rewarding and productive relationships based on voluntary cooperation.

CHAPTER THREE

OBSTACLES TO CLEAR THINKING ABOUT GOVERNMENT

Listen carefully to people discussing or debating political issues. You will hear many fallacies or obstacles that get in the way of clear thinking. Following is a brief discussion of six frequently encountered fallacies.

THE UTOPIAN FALLACY

"Utopia" refers to a perfect society, where everyone gets everything they want all the time and nothing ever goes wrong. No such place has ever existed. But opponents of liberty hold Utopia up as a standard. They argue that liberty does not guarantee that everyone will get everything they want. Some will be sick, hungry, or disappointed. There will still be murderers, thieves, rapists, and other criminals. Because liberty does not *guarantee* Utopia, they argue, we should reject liberty and embrace government control.

It is true that no advocate of liberty can guarantee Utopia.

So what?

No advocate of *any* political view can guarantee Utopia.

Utopia is not one of the options.

Utopia is simply not available. Let's examine the available options and choose the best.

There are three options in politics in America today. The first option is the status quo: the government and politics of the last 50 years and a continuation of trends developed during those years.

Most Americans today express a great dissatisfaction with the status quo.

The second option is to move toward even larger government and more government involvement in more aspects of our lives. That option is inevitably accompanied by increased taxes, a declining economy, and loss of liberty. Most Americans find the ever-larger, more intrusive government option even less appealing than the status quo.

The third option is to move toward reducing the size of government, reducing its involvement in our personal and business affairs, and reducing its costs (thus reducing taxes). Making such reductions would increase your freedom and your control over your own life. Upon reflection, most Americans prefer this option.

It bears repeating: *Utopia is not an option.* When you hear someone object to the idea of greater freedom by saying, for example, "You cannot guarantee that all children will get a good education if we repeal compulsory school attendance laws," that's the Utopian fallacy. A better question would be: "What system will allow the greatest number of children to get the best education?"

THE "PANG" (People Are No Good) PREMISE

This fallacy is found in almost every argument for government regulation of peoples' lives. The unstated premise is that people are weak, stupid, helpless, incompetent, dishonest, and dangerous to themselves and others. They need a nanny! Some examples: Social Security is necessary because people would not provide for their own future. The draft is necessary because not enough people are willing to defend America. Drug laws are necessary because without them we would be a nation of stoned-out addicts. Compulsory school attendance laws are necessary because parents wouldn't educate their children. And so on.

The PANG premise has a huge logical hole in it. It ignores the fact that those very same weak, stupid, helpless, incompetent, dishonest, and dangerous people would be the ones running government! After all, government is no more than the collection of people — politicians and bureaucrats — who operate it. If the

PANG premise were valid, the last thing we'd want is a powerful government managed by such people, running our lives. As one wag put it, "If people are basically good, you don't need a government; if people are basically evil, you don't dare have one."

The truth is, most people, most of the time, act morally. They don't lie, cheat, steal, rape, or murder. Mostly, we act on the principle of respect for other human beings, recognizing that they have the right to control their own affairs, and expecting that they, in turn, will deal with us peacefully and honestly.

One other comment about the PANG Premise: did you ever notice that the people who cite it always seem to exclude *themselves* from the category of people who are weak, stupid, helpless, incompetent, dishonest, and dangerous?

THE REIFICATION FALLACY

"Reification" is a fancy word for treating a concept or a label as something that actually exists. The mistake is in forgetting that the concept or label doesn't really exist, only people do. "Government" does not exist as a thing separate from the people in it. Certainly it is necessary to have a term like "government," just as we have terms like church, school, army, union, corporation, and family. But, none of these labels (groups) has an existence apart from, or greater than, the individuals in it.

Whenever you hear someone discussing what the government, or the bureaucrats, or the big corporations, or the unions did, always ask, "Which *individuals* did what things?" Only individuals can act. And, of course, individuals should be held responsible for the consequences of their actions.

One reason people use this fallacy is to depersonalize other people they want to mistreat. It is easy to call for heavy taxation of the "big corporations." It is not so easy to call for reducing the dividends of the pensioners, widows, and orphans who depend on pension funds that own shares in the same big corporations.

Another motivation behind using this fallacy is to buttress the argument that you, an individual, are less important than abstract groups such as "society." You, the argument goes, should sacrifice your interests for the benefit of the larger group. But the group is merely a collection of individuals.

Have you noticed that it is always *you* who must sacrifice to the others — not the other way around?

THE FREE LUNCH FALLACY

One of the most basic principles of economics has been stated in the following charmingly ungrammatical fashion: "There ain't no such thing as a free lunch" (TANSTAAFL). The proposition is true and indisputable. Unfortunately, where political matters are concerned, many people seem to believe there *is* a free lunch. That is, they think they *can* get something for nothing.

Frequently we hear of free education or free medical care. Your property tax bill or federal income tax return will demonstrate that these things are not free. Neither teachers nor doctors work for free. Government employees generally receive good salaries. The source of payment for all government services is the earnings and property of taxpayers — you and me.

Anyone receiving something from government does so at the expense of other hard-working Americans. The only question is whether people receiving government "benefits" will pay for them, or whether they — with the assistance of government force — can make others pay. Either way, someone always pays; nothing is free.

THE FALLACY OF LEGISLATIVE OMNICOMPETENCE

Here's another one of those fancy words. "Omnicompetence" is just a short way of saying: competent to do everything imaginable. This fallacy is based on a twofold error: that government is competent to deal effectively with every problem — and that it should do so.

The more fundamental part of the fallacy is to believe that every aspect of human activity is appropriately subject to government control. That's the exact *opposite* of the principles on which this country was founded. It is the principle of totalitarianism.

Government has no justification to act except to assist individuals in defending themselves from those who would violate their rights. I have no right to use force to control the lives and activities of others — and no one in government can claim the right to do so based on a consent I cannot morally give.

The more obvious part of the fallacy can be seen in the fact that government doesn't work. Using the coercion of law to achieve social ends never leads to the results sought and inevitably has other unintended consequences. Some examples: The federal government's War on Poverty has spent over $9 trillion, yet there are as many people in poverty as when it started 40 years ago. Billions of dollars spent by the federal government on education has been accompanied by declining student performance and increased violence in schools. Thirty years after the government launched its War on Drugs, 80% of high school juniors and seniors say marijuana is easy to obtain.

One major reason that government doesn't work is that no person's "good idea" makes it through the legislative process without major modifications from every affected interest group. The resulting law will be something no one really wanted. Further, no one can predict how people will change their conduct in reaction to it, as they inevitably do. So what happens in the real world is usually very different than the results intended by those who proposed the law.

THE VICTIMLESS CRIME LAW FALLACY

This fallacy is the best example of the one discussed immediately above. Many believe that people will stop engaging in peaceful activities if only legislators would pass a law making those activities a crime. (Unfortunately, about 50% of our current law enforcement efforts and expenses are wasted on enforcing laws that penalize peaceful, honest conduct.)

The Prohibition experiment in America is instructive. In 1920, a constitutional amendment went into effect that prohibited the production and sale of alcoholic beverages. Supporters of the law said it would stop people from drinking and liberate America from the negative consequences of alcohol. The results were disastrous. Prohibition spawned organized crime gangs and criminals like Al "Scarface" Capone. The price of illegal booze increased, creating profit opportunities for anyone willing to engage in criminal activity. Large quantities of alcohol were smuggled over the border from Canada. Criminal profiteers corrupted the criminal justice system, buying off police, courts, and jailers. "Speakeasies" — illegal, underground bars — did booming business in every major city. Innocent people were caught in the crossfire as violent criminal gangs fought each other in turf wars. Meanwhile, tens of millions of Americans flouted the law and continued to drink. Admitting defeat, politicians finally repealed Prohibition in 1933.

This general pattern repeats itself any time government turns a peaceful, honest activity into a crime. People do not quit buying products and services just because of the risk of criminal prosecution. As a result, "black markets" to supply the now-illegal demand grow and flourish. Such illegal markets have most, if not all, of the dangerous characteristics of the illegal market for alcohol that developed during Prohibition.

It is amusing to hear people argue that, if there were no drug laws, millions of Americans would suddenly decide to smoke marijuana or snort cocaine. The fact is, 25 million to 40 million Americans already do so — even though it is a crime. Even more significantly, states that have largely decriminalized marijuana possession for personal use have seen no dramatic surge in the drug's popularity.

Nonetheless, we hear similar absurdities repeated in arguments for other laws that exist — and do not work. We are earnestly told that without laws against immigration, thousands from Mexico and Central America would come here. Without laws against prostitution, people would buy and sell sexual services. Without laws against carrying concealed weapons, criminals would carry guns.

Supporters of victimless crime laws never seem to learn. Trying to suppress peaceful conduct with criminal penalties never works. Victimless crime laws do not *stop* people from engaging in forbidden activities, and repealing such laws generally does not encourage more people to *start* engaging in formerly forbidden activities.

CONCLUSION

People believe many fallacies and mistaken ideas about politics. The foregoing discussion involves six frequently encountered fallacies and obstacles to clear thinking. Stay alert and you will detect these, and others, often. In any discussion of ten minutes or more, each fallacy is likely to appear more than once.

Keep this in mind. If an argument is based on a fallacy, it is either partly or completely invalid. In politics, skepticism toward those who employ fallacious arguments is valuable protection for your pocketbook — and for your freedom.

CHAPTER FOUR

THE DEVELOPMENT OF LIBERTARIANISM AS AN AMERICAN POLITICAL MOVEMENT

In 1776 a small group of British subjects living on the eastern seaboard of North America decided to break the chains of British tyranny. They gave notice to the world that they were doing so, and the reasons why, in the most important political document in human history, the Declaration of Independence, written by Thomas Jefferson. The Declaration of Independence states:

> *We hold these truths to be self-evident, that all men are created equal; that they are endowed by their Creator with certain unalienable rights; that among these rights are life, liberty, and the pursuit of happiness. That, to secure these rights, governments are instituted among men, deriving their just powers from the consent of the governed; that, whenever any form of government becomes destructive of these ends, it is the right of the people to alter or abolish it, and to institute a new government, laying its foundation on such principles, and organizing its powers in such form, as to them shall seem most likely to effect their safety and happiness.*
>
> *Prudence, indeed, will dictate that governments long established should not be changed for light and transient causes; and, accordingly, all experience hath shown, that mankind are more disposed to suffer, while evils are sufferable, than to right themselves by abolishing the forms to which they are accustomed. But, when a long train of abuses and usurpations, pursuing invariably the same object, evinces a*

*design to reduce them under absolute despotism, it is their
duty to throw off such governments, and to provide new guards
for their future security.*

These magnificent words from the Declaration state three fundamental propositions. First, human beings have rights which are derived from the natural order of the universe and the characteristics of human beings. That is, humans have a specific nature that is the basis for the rights we have.

Second, the institution of government is something created by mankind to protect these rights. Thus, rights do not come from government; instead, people create governments to protect their fundamental rights.

Third, when government fails as a protector of rights, people have not only the right but the *duty* to change or abolish it.

NATURAL RIGHTS; PROPERTY RIGHTS

Libertarianism is grounded in the "natural rights" tradition in Western culture. The signers of the Declaration of Independence were familiar with and strongly influenced by this natural rights tradition. Philosopher John Locke was a major contributor to their thinking.

Locke laid the foundation for our understanding of property. He showed us that "homesteading" is the basis for property rights. As men go out into nature as yet unclaimed, an individual must "mix his labor with the land" in order to establish a just claim of ownership. The obvious example would be to clear unowned land of stones and brush for farming.

Once acquired, property was subject to the control of the owner. That owner could use it for his own purposes and, most importantly, could exclude others from it. The concept of private property continues to be of crucial importance in the libertarian political philosophy.

CONSTITUTION AND BILL OF RIGHTS

After their successful Revolution, the thirteen new states in North America created a level of government separate from their state governments, establishing it with the Articles of Confederation. Subsequently, the states replaced the Articles of Confederation with the Constitution, the charter for today's United States government.

The American people were justifiably concerned about creating a powerful national government that might try to oppress them. So the Constitution they approved created a national government with strictly specified and limited powers.

The people also knew that governments tend to grow and become more powerful over time. So, as a condition to ratification of the Constitution, the people demanded a Bill of Rights to guard against future infringements on their rights. The Bill of Rights shows how determined the people were that the new national government not interfere in the areas of their lives that were precious and sacred to them. The Bill of Rights is a list of "government shall not..." restrictions.

Article One: Congress shall make no law respecting an establishment of religion, or prohibiting the free exercise thereof; or abridging the freedom of speech, or of the press; or the right of the people peaceably to assemble, and to petition the government for a redress of grievances.

Article Two: A well-regulated militia being necessary to the security of a free State, the right of the people to keep and bear arms shall not be infringed.

Article Three: No soldier shall, in time of peace be quartered in any house, without the consent of the owner, nor in time of war but in a manner to be prescribed by law.

Article Four: The right of the people to be secure in their persons, houses, papers, and effects, against unreasonable searches and seizures, shall not be violated, and no warrants shall issue, but upon probable cause, supported by oath or affirmation, and particularly describing the place to be searched and the person or things to be seized.

Article Five: No person shall be held to answer for a capital, or otherwise infamous crime, unless on a presentment or indictment of a Grand Jury, except in cases arising in the land or naval forces, or in the militia, when in actual service in time of war or public danger; nor shall any person be subject for the same offense to be twice put in jeopardy of life or limb; nor shall be compelled in any criminal case to be a witness against himself, nor be deprived of life, liberty, or property, without due process of law; nor shall private property be taken for public use, without just compensation.

Article Six: In all criminal prosecutions the accused shall enjoy the right to a speedy and public trial, by an impartial jury of the State and district wherein the crime shall have been committed, which district shall have been previously ascertained by law, and to be informed of the nature and cause of the accusation; to be confronted with the witness against him; to have compulsory process for obtaining witnesses in his favor, and to have the assistance of counsel for his defense.

Article Seven: In suits at common law, where the value in controversy shall exceed twenty dollars, the right of trial by jury shall be preserved, and no fact tried by a jury shall be otherwise reexamined in any court of the United States, than according to the rules of the common law.

Article Eight: Excessive bail shall not be required, nor excessive fines imposed, nor cruel and unusual punishments inflicted.

Article Nine: The enumeration in the Constitution of certain rights shall not be construed to deny or disparage others retained by the people.

Article Ten: The powers not delegated to the United States by the Constitution, nor prohibited by it to the States, are reserved to the States respectively or to the people.

The Ninth and Tenth Amendments confirm that the people have *all* the rights and power — and that the U.S. government has no powers, except those explicitly granted to it by the people and expressly stated in the Constitution.

Unfortunately, in the centuries since the adoption of the Constitution, Supreme Court decisions have essentially reversed these important constitutional principles. Today, one must point to a specific limitation on government in the Bill of Rights to have even a hope of curtailing federal or state encroachment.

NON-INTERVENTIONISM, THE FREE TRADE MOVEMENT, AND ABOLITIONISTS

A look at the early days of the American republic reveals an abundance of libertarian policies and activities.

One nineteenth-century government policy most in accord with today's libertarian views was a foreign policy of non-intervention. As Thomas Jefferson succinctly explained it: "Peace, commerce and honest friendship with all nations; entangling alliances with none." From the administration of George Washington to that of James Monroe, the U.S. government rarely intervened in the affairs of other countries, refused to enter into military alliances, and encouraged free international trade.

This beneficial policy began to unravel in 1823 with the Monroe Doctrine, which stated that the U.S. would not allow European powers to interfere in the Western Hemisphere. By the end of the nineteenth century, non-interventionism was largely forgotten, as the U.S. government began to meddle militarily in Central America and the Pacific.

Free-market economics was another major libertarian concept that held sway in the fledgling United States. Adam Smith's book, *The Wealth of Nations*, published in 1776, is usually credited with launching the modern science of economics, based on markets, prices, production, and so forth. Other writers and theorists contributed to this tradition, but Smith's work was most widely known in the English-speaking world. In the early days of the United States, there was almost no government regulation of business or banks, people valued hard work and enterprise, and taxes and tariffs were low. As a result, the nation prospered.

During the first half of the 19th century, free-market economists who advocated elimination of trade barriers between nations were in the ascendancy in the Western world. British Parliamentary leaders Richard Cobden and John Bright led the movement for free international trade and demolished the arguments for protectionism. Free trade was, and still is, a powerful inducement to peaceful relationships between countries. As the French economist Frederic Bastiat put it: "If goods are not allowed to cross international borders, soldiers will."

Finally, a significant libertarian movement during the first half of the 19th century was abolitionism — the campaign to eradicate slavery in the United States. Abolitionists, who, it could be argued, were that era's libertarians, made the case that slavery trampled on the natural human right to be free.

THE CIVIL WAR

The great and welcome result of the Civil War was the end of slavery. Less well known are the anti-libertarian elements introduced during that war. Both the North and the South used conscription to build their fighting forces. President Abraham Lincoln suspended the right of *habeas corpus* (the right to go before a court to appeal an unlawful imprisonment) and had anti-war dissenters jailed. The first income tax was imposed in 1862. Although these violations of liberty were dropped after the war, they laid a foundation for later incursions.

Most significantly, the Civil War itself eliminated, by force of arms, the concept that the people of a sovereign state could choose to secede from the Union. Nowhere in the Constitution is the federal government granted the power to prevent secession.

FREE-MARKET ECONOMICS

The rise of Marxism in the nineteenth century was a powerful counterforce to libertarianism. Even so, libertarian theoretical work continued. Most important was the development of the "Austrian" school of economics which, on every issue, showed that economic theory must be grounded in the actions of individuals. Consequently, individuals must be free for economic prosperity to result. The political implications of that insight are obvious.

Ludwig von Mises was the most significant of the Austrians. In 1922, Mises published one of his important works, *Socialism*, in which he demonstrated the impossibility of efficient economic calculation in a socialist economy. Mises showed that any centrally directed economy must fail. Without a free market for goods and services, there is no market-pricing mechanism to tell producers and entrepreneurs what consumers most desire, or how to efficiently allocate resources. Although Mises was ignored by mainstream economists and politicians, he was later proven correct by the disastrous consequences of socialism in Eastern Europe, the Soviet Union, and around the world.

THE DEPRESSION AND WORLD WAR II

The influence of libertarian thought in America was at its lowest during the 1930s Great Depression and the 1940s war period. One myth in American history is that the collapse of the stock market in 1929 and the subsequent Depression were the result of capitalism's failure. The historical evidence clearly contradicts this. The U.S. government's inflationary monetary policies during the 1920s and other U.S. government actions — such as erecting international trade barriers and making the private possession of gold illegal — simply delayed the economic corrections that would have occurred if the government had not intervened in the economy. Murray Rothbard's *America's Great Depression* (1963) effectively rebuts the notion that the Depression was caused by free-market economics gone wrong.

As Randolph Bourne wrote: "War is the health of the state."

During World War II, as in all wars, the U.S. government grew dramatically. Controls over personal and economic activities increased. Libertarian ideals of individual rights, respect for personal rights, due process, free markets, and non-intervention in foreign wars were swept aside. Libertarian voices were among the few raised to defend the rights of Japanese-Americans when the U.S. government forced them into internment camps without due process and without concern for the legal presumption of innocence.

POST-WORLD WAR II ECONOMISTS AND AYN RAND

After World War II, the libertarian movement consisted of a small handful of free-market scholars, among them economists Mises, Henry Hazlitt, Murray Rothbard, and Friedrich Hayek (later to win a Nobel Prize in economics); novelist Ayn Rand (*The Fountainhead, Atlas Shrugged*); Leonard Read, founder of the Foundation for Economic Education; and R.C. Hoiles, publisher of the Freedom Newspapers.

In addition to the Austrian School of economics, a new free-market approach to economics was developing at the University of Chicago, led by Milton Friedman, another Nobel Prize recipient — now known as the "Chicago School."

The number of people who came to call themselves "libertarians" during the 1940s and 1950s grew at a slow but steady pace. But no organized libertarian political movement yet existed. In the 1960s, a combination of factors fertilized the ground for the subsequent growth of an explicitly libertarian political movement.

Ayn Rand published her major novel, *Atlas Shrugged*, in 1957. This novel sparked a movement among young intellectuals to explore further her individualist philosophy — called Objectivism — and to challenge establishment political views. By the early 1960s, groups on college campuses and elsewhere were eagerly studying Rand's novels and debating their philosophical implications.

During the 1960s, many young people came to disagree with the U.S. military involvement in Vietnam. Although a significant percentage of the anti-Vietnam War movement leaders were leftists and socialists, many shared the libertarian concern for human rights. Many also expressed concern about the effects of President Richard Nixon's domestic security measures on personal liberties. Libertarians were then relatively few in number, but they spoke out against the war, opposing the draft and protesting the CIA's and FBI's domestic surveillance of American citizens.

VIETNAM PLUS NIXON LEADS TO YOUTH COALITION FOR FREEDOM

A youth coalition for liberty developed during the 1960s and early 1970s. Many young people came to libertarian views by study of free-market economics and the writings of Ayn Rand. Others were involved in anti-Vietnam War activity or in the civil rights movement. They believed that individuals have the right to live their lives free from police harassment for their skin color, hair length, clothing styles, or living arrangements. People in both groups were not comfortable with traditional "right-wing" or "left-wing" labels. They finally came together near the close of the 1960s.

Ironically, President Nixon was an impetus for the birth of the modern libertarian movement. As the 1970s dawned, government harassment of anti-Vietnam War organizations at Nixon's direction was well known, certainly among its victims. In 1971, Nixon imposed wage and price controls, demolishing among many any lingering hope that the Republican Party would ever reduce government intervention in the market. A group of young people committed to liberty gathered and decided that the American political system needed a new political party which promoted freedom for everyone, on all issues, all the time.

The founding convention of the Libertarian Party was held in December 1971 in Colorado Springs. The new organization adopted a Statement of Principles, which reads in part:

> *We hold that all individuals have the right to exercise sole dominion over their own lives, and have the right to live in whatever manner they choose, so long as they do not forcibly*

interfere with the right of others to live in whatever manner they choose.

Governments throughout history have regularly operated on the opposite principle, that the State has the right to dispose of the lives of individuals and the fruits of their labor. Even within the United States, all political parties other than our own grant to government the right to regulate the lives of individuals and seize the fruits of their labor without their consent.

We, on the contrary, deny the right of any government to do these things, and hold that where governments exist, they must not violate the rights of any individual: namely (1) the right to life – accordingly we support prohibition of the initiation of physical force against others; (2) the right to liberty of speech and action – accordingly we oppose all attempts by governments to abridge the freedom of speech and press, as well as government censorship in any form; and (3) the right to property – accordingly we oppose all government interference with private property, such as confiscation, nationalization, and eminent domain, and support the prohibition of robbery, trespass, fraud, and misrepresentation.

The ideas expressed in the Declaration of Independence and Bill of Rights (both quoted earlier in this chapter) and in this Statement of Principles are a clear guide to the modern libertarian movement's thinking and goals.

In 1972, John Hospers, the first Libertarian Party presidential candidate, was on the ballot in two states and received approximately 2,500 votes. Since that modest beginning, the Libertarian Party has grown to become arguably America's largest and most successful third party, with organizations in every state. Hundreds of Libertarian candidates have been elected to state and local offices.

Libertarian political activists have been active in many of the important political battles of the past three decades. They played a major role in the success of anti-tax efforts such as California's Proposition 13. Libertarians have been prominently involved in the term-limits movement, which seeks to make "professional politicians" a thing of the past. In 1996, libertarians supported the successful "medical marijuana" initiatives in California and Arizona. They also endorsed the California Civil Rights Initiative, which ended ethnic and gender quotas in government education, hiring, and contracting. In 1999, the Libertarian Party played a major role in defeating the proposed federal "Know Your Customer" regulations, which would have required banks to report their customers' financial affairs to the government. Libertarian policies such as privatization, deregulation, choice in education, ending the War on Drugs, free trade, and tolerance for lifestyle choice are embraced by more and more Americans.

Partisan libertarian political action is not confined to the Libertarian Party. Libertarian political activists formed the Republican Liberty Caucus and the Democratic Freedom Caucus, which work to push those parties in a more libertarian direction. There are also libertarians who are not involved in any political party.

AN INFLUENTIAL MOVEMENT

In the United States, libertarianism has become a multifaceted movement. Libertarian-oriented think tanks play an increasingly important role in shaping public opinion. Organizations such as the Cato Institute, the Institute for Humane Studies, the Reason Foundation, Citizens for a Sound Economy, the Property and Environmental Research Center (PERC), the National Center for Policy Analysis, the Heartland Institute, and the Pacific Institute for Public Policy Research — to name but a few — help bring libertarian ideas and policy proposals to voters and decision-makers.

But Libertarian influence goes beyond scholarly think tanks. *Reason* magazine is an influential and respected monthly publication that explores the application of libertarian ideas to current events and culture. An increasing number of libertarian scholars hold teaching positions in colleges and universities. We now see judges with libertarian attitudes on state and federal benches. Dozens of famous celebrities — including Clint Eastwood,

Dave Barry, John Stossel, and Kurt Russell — publicly identify themselves as "libertarian." There are even libertarian musicians, including Neil Peart of Rush, bluesman Jimmie Vaughan, and country singer Dwight Yoakam.

The publisher of this book, the Advocates for Self-Government (founded in 1985), brings the ideas of liberty to the public, teaches libertarians how to become more effective communicators, and publishes the World's Smallest Political Quiz (see Chapter 5).

Meanwhile, libertarianism has also become an influential international movement. Groups such as the International Society for Individual Liberty (ISIL) work to promotes libertarianism in foreign countries. According to one estimate, there are now libertarian (or libertarian-friendly) think tanks, organizations, and political parties in more than 100 nations.

CHAPTER FIVE

THE LIBERTARIAN DIFFERENCE

Libertarianism differs substantially from the political philosophies of liberalism and conservatism.

All libertarian positions derive from, and are consistent with, basic principles. Libertarianism begins with self-ownership. Each person owns himself or herself. Therefore, each person has the absolute right to control his or her own life, body, speech, actions, and honestly acquired property.

Every person has these rights. Therefore, every one of us must also respect the equal rights of every other person.

An individual has the right to defend his own life and property, but cannot violate another's rights when doing so. Further, no one can authorize another person to violate someone else's rights. I cannot authorize my representative in government to violate the rights of another — no matter how much good I think that might accomplish. Because of this obligation to respect the rights of others, no one can make any legitimate claim on the person, earnings, or property of any other individual. Each of us is responsible for himself or herself (and, of course, others for whom we choose to accept responsibility, such as family and friends).

From this foundation, one can derive a libertarian position consistent with those principles on almost any issue.

CONFUSING POLITICAL LABELS

Consider the labels "liberal" and "conservative." While liberals tend to have some broad areas of agreement among themselves — as do conservatives — those labels cannot reliably tell you how a person will stand on any particular issue. Neither can the labels "Democrat" or "Republican."

Consider those partisan labels first. The Democratic and Republican parties adopt platforms at every presidential nominating convention. Every four years they can take positions that flatly contradict a stance they've taken before. Either party can come down on either side of most issues, depending on changing public opinion or the whims of their presidential candidates.

The same is true for liberals and conservatives. Any individual liberal or conservative may be for or against a particular tax, a proposed educational "reform," foreign military intervention, a new federal welfare initiative, censorship, a government surveillance program, affirmative action, or a host of other issues.

The cause of this uncertainty is simple: Liberals and conservatives have no philosophical objection to the use of government force; they only (sometimes) disagree where and why it should be applied. They frequently *both* support the use of government power, but for different reasons. For example, a liberal might support censorship to eradicate racist language; a conservative to fight pornographic images. A liberal might endorse government surveillance to track "right-wing extremists"; a conservative to thwart illegal immigrants. A liberal might favor a new federal program to aid the homeless; a conservative to help big business. A liberal might favor mandatory "national service" to help the poor; a conservative the draft to build the military. The list goes on.

By contrast, libertarians *always* act with respect for every person's rights. Libertarians *always* hold that people in government must do their jobs without violating any individual's rights.

Unlike liberals and conservatives, libertarians understand that the only way politicians can dole out favors is if those resources are first stolen from other citizens. This is why libertarians advocate an end to coercive taxation as a method of financing government functions, and call for replacing it with voluntary financing methods. That's why libertarians seek to reduce the size and scope of government, and confine it to assisting citizens in defending their rights against those who might violate them.

Because of this unwavering support for individual rights,

libertarians are far more consistent about limiting the role of government in our lives than are people who describe themselves with the traditional labels "liberal" and "conservative."

A REPLACEMENT FOR THE OUTDATED LEFT-RIGHT SPECTRUM

People frequently ask: Are libertarians left-wing or right-wing? Liberal or conservative? The answer is neither. It is a mistake to attempt to locate libertarians on the "left-right spectrum," because that traditional method of measuring political beliefs is so incomplete and simplistic. Curiously, many political analysts and commentators seem blind to this defect — even as they struggle to try to shoehorn every variety of political belief into this traditional scheme.

The following "Diamond Chart" displays (and explains) a more accurate spectrum of political positions. It clearly shows there is more to the political map than just "right versus left." It does so by measuring where people stand on two crucial measures — personal liberty and economic liberty. The chart is based on an analysis of politics developed by Libertarian Party founder David Nolan, and further expanded by Marshall Fritz, founder of the Advocates for Self-Government.

WORLD'S SMALLEST POLITICAL QUIZ

Use the chart below to see where you fit on the expanded political map. Begin by answering the following 10 questions. For each statement, circle A for Agree, M for Maybe, or D for Disagree.

How do you stand on PERSONAL issues?

	20	10	0
Government should not censor speech, press, media or Internet.	A	M	D
Military service should be voluntary. There should be no draft.	A	M	D
There should be no laws regarding sex between consenting adults.	A	M	D
Repeal laws prohibiting adult possession and use of drugs.	A	M	D
There should be no National ID card.	A	M	D

SCORING: 20 for every A, 10 for every M, and O for every D: _____

How do you stand on ECONOMIC issues?

	20	10	0
End "corporate welfare." No government handouts to business.	A	M	D
End government barriers to international free trade.	A	M	D
Let people control their own retirement: privatize Social Security.	A	M	D
Replace government welfare with private charity.	A	M	D
Cut taxes and government spending by 50% or more.	A	M	D

SCORING: 20 for every A, 10 for every M, and O for every D: _____

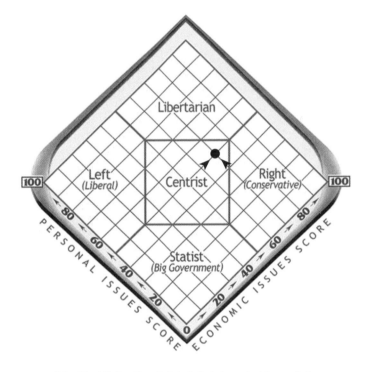

(The World's Smallest Political Quiz is used with permission from the Advocates for Self-Government.)

Now find your place on the chart. Mark your PERSONAL score on the lower-left scale, your ECONOMIC score on the lower-right. Then follow the grid lines until they meet at your political position. Your score shows who most agrees with you in politics, and where you agree and disagree with other political philosophies. (See example of 50% personal and 70% economic.)

You can also plot the political identity of politicians and public figures based on how you think they would answer the questions. For instance, former President Ronald Reagan and radio commentator Rush Limbaugh would probably fall in the "right" quadrant; U.S. Senator Hillary Clinton and radio host Al Franken in the "left." In the "centrist" section you might find U.S. Senator John McCain and radio talk show host Dennis Prager; in the "libertarian" quadrant, U.S. Rep. Ron Paul and TV newsman John Stossel. Tyrants like Josef Stalin, Adolf Hitler, and Fidel Castro are clearly at the very bottom in the "statist" quadrant.

ECONOMIC AND PERSONAL LIBERTIES

The brilliant insight of the World's Smallest Political Quiz is that it divides human affairs into two major areas: economic and personal.

Economic issues involve your money: decisions about employment, trade, investments, and business. Personal issues involve what you do with your body: choices about what you read, eat, drink, smoke or with whom you choose to associate.

The important question for determining a political position is how much liberty a person advocates in each of these two areas. Or, conversely, what percentage of control a person wants government to exercise over our personal and economic activities.

We can see from the Diamond Chart that liberals advocate a relatively high degree of personal liberty. Concurrently, liberals call for a good deal of government control over people's economic activities. Liberals tend to assume that we are competent to run our private lives, but we need to be tightly controlled when engaged in business, lest we exploit other people or become too wealthy.

Typically, conservatives reverse the liberal's emphasis. Conservatives advocate a relatively high level of economic freedom; that is, low taxes and less government regulation of business. Concurrently, they call for less personal liberty. To conservatives, we are capable of freely engaging in commercial activity but need to be watched in our private lives, lest we sin or otherwise act irresponsibly.

Libertarians are found in the upper quadrant of the chart. That's the location for all who advocate a high degree of *both* economic *and* personal liberty. Libertarians believe that people have the right to freely engage in both commercial and private activities. Libertarians consistently uphold the right of individuals to control their own lives in all respects.

Those in total opposition to libertarians are located in the lower quadrant of the chart. They are referred to as "statists." These people believe that virtually all human activity should be subject to government control and that any significant level of personal or economic liberty is dangerous. Statists aren't necessarily undemocratic; many believe that government represents the collective "will of the people." However, at the very bottom of the quadrant, statism turns into tyranny. There you'll find the Marxists, socialists, communists, and fascists who believe in absolute government control over the individual.

Centrists pick and choose among issues, and do not consistently support either freedom or government control. Their stance tends to depend on how they feel about a particular issue.

LIBERTARIAN POSITIONS: PRINCIPLED AND CONSISTENT

Libertarianism is not some variant of left-wing or liberal thinking, nor some variant of right-wing or conservative thinking. Nor is it a *combination* of left and right. It is a unique and consistent political philosophy.

On the chart, libertarians share a common border with both liberals and conservatives. It is not unusual for liberals to take the libertarian position on certain personal liberties issues. Nor is it unusual for conservatives to take the libertarian position on some economic issues. As we've noted, liberals and conservatives sometimes support government control — and sometimes don't. By contrast, all libertarian positions are derived from the basic principles of self-ownership and respect for the equal rights of others. The same consistent, principled approach is not true for other political groups.

That is why you cannot predict the position of any Democrat,

Republican, liberal, or conservative on any given issue at any time. They have no consistent way to deal with issues because they have no fundamental philosophical principles. The best you can do is compile a list of positions they hold on issues and check from time to time for any changes.

Because libertarians do have a basic set of principles, you know that a libertarian will *always* come down on the side of any issue which maximizes personal liberty and responsibility — and which reduces government control over the individual.

The libertarian looks at the people involved in any situation and asks whether they are dealing with each other in a peaceful, voluntary, and honest way. If they are, then no one should bring force into the situation. And no uninvited outside party, including government, should bring force into the situation. To do so will violate someone's rights.

This does not mean that one should decline to offer assistance, help, or advice to others in need. Indeed, since libertarians believe in private charity — rather than government welfare — libertarians heartily endorse the idea of offering voluntary assistance to people who might need help. (People always have the choice to accept or decline such assistance.) But the political issue is this: When is it legitimate for the government to use force? We must continually ask ourselves that very important question. Libertarians will always answer: Only to defend the rights of the citizen.

Ultimately, that belief is what separates libertarians from any other political philosophy.

CHAPTER SIX

LIBERTARIAN ANALYSIS OF THE ISSUES

To examine any issue from the libertarian point of view, we must consider two elements: the "moral" and the "practical."

THE MORAL ELEMENT

The moral portion of the analysis requires that we consider the conduct of the people in the situation. Are they dealing with each other in a peaceful, voluntary, and honest manner? If they are, then no one is violating the rights of any other. In such cases, it is immoral for anyone to introduce force into the situation, no matter how much good he thinks he could achieve by coercing people into changing their conduct.

If one person uses force (or the threat of it) against another person, that aggressor is violating the rights of the other. Such *aggressive* use of force should be stopped. And just as it is moral and proper for an individual to use force for self-defense, it is moral to use government force to assist people whose rights are being violated by an aggressor.

To a libertarian, the answer to the moral question is primary. Determining the right (moral) course of action is of utmost importance. Traditional politicians seldom question whether government force is being used properly (to assist citizens in defending their rights) or improperly (to violate the citizens' rights). A libertarian will *always* raise that question. A libertarian will *always* argue against the improper use of government force.

We have all become accustomed to politicians and political commentators limiting themselves to practical considerations. So it sounds odd when someone, usually a libertarian, questions whether a proposal to use government force is morally justified. It sounds odd to hear someone say: "If it is illegal or immoral for a private individual to do something, then it is illegal or immoral for the government to do it."

It is rare when the moral issue becomes part of the general public discussion. The morality of the military draft is one of those rare instances. During the Vietnam War (and even today with the legal obligation to register for the draft still on the books), people debated whether it was moral to impose criminal penalties on young men who refused to register or be drafted. Before the Civil War, libertarians of that day (abolitionists) challenged the moral legitimacy of an established legal institution (slavery).

Libertarians want to see the moral question — the right of each individual to live his life in any peaceful way he chooses — made a part of the debate on *every* issue.

THE PRACTICAL ELEMENT

What do we mean by the practical element? This involves considerations and predictions of what people will do in response to a law, regulation, or government policy.

The practical analysis only asks whether, if a specific law is passed, people would do what the legislators intend. Consider some examples. If the law imposes criminal penalties on employers who hire illegal aliens, will employers begin to discriminate against all immigrants, legal and illegal? If Congress cuts taxes, will businesses produce more? If the minimum wage law is eliminated, will employers hire more unskilled teenagers, or will all employees see their wages go down? If ownership of handguns is made illegal, will people willingly give up their guns, or will a larger black market in guns develop? If criminal penalties for possession of marijuana were eliminated, would it reduce crime, or would it induce millions more to try marijuana? If trade barriers were repealed, would it hurt or help the U.S. economy?

LIBERTY WORKS; GOVERNMENT DOESN'T

One of the nagging questions in many people's minds, even if they find the morality of freedom appealing, is whether it is practical. *Does freedom work?* If there were fewer governmental restrictions on their actions, would people deal effectively with the problems in their lives? Or in the absence of government's coercive supervision, would people make a terrible mess of their lives?

Libertarians work for freedom because it is *practical* as well as *moral.* The more freedom, the greater opportunity you will have to achieve the goals and values *you* choose. Libertarians believe that you know what is best for you. You know what your goals, dreams, and values are. And you know these things infinitely better than do government officials.

This is a good place to remind ourselves of the Utopian fallacy. The choice is not between Utopia and liberty. *Utopia is not an option.*

The choice is between liberty and coercive government control of your affairs. There is no middle ground. Either *you* get to decide, or politicians and bureaucrats get to decide. If politicians and bureaucrats get the power to make those decisions, then you must do as they say or be punished.

Americans are finally catching on to the fact that government doesn't work. Government regulations and programs are invariably expensive and intrusive, and they fail to accomplish their intended goals. In fact, they almost always lead to unintended consequences — usually bad. Liberty works remarkably well by comparison.

* * * *

The following chapters contain a series of brief discussions on current political issues. These discussions proceed from a libertarian point of view and the analyses will contain both moral and practical considerations.

CHAPTER SEVEN

FOREIGN POLICY, FREE TRADE, NATIONAL DEFENSE, AND TERRORISM

*Peace, commerce, and honest friendship with
all nations; entangling alliances with none.*
— Thomas Jefferson

Libertarian foreign policy can be summed up in this phrase: neutrality, free trade, and a federal government limited to defending Americans in America. This is what the Founders of America established with the Constitution.

Unfortunately, for more than a century, our government has followed a policy of foreign interventionism. It has implemented legal restrictions on peaceful trade and travel. It has lied time after time about national defense matters, often taking the U.S. into war on false pretenses. It has made the United States a tempting target for terrorists. Congress, which alone has the power to declare war under the Constitution, has defaulted, repeatedly allowing the president to send the military into conflicts in foreign lands. The costs of this interventionism have been huge — in terms of lives lost, increased threats to the nation, and growing limitations on American liberty.

In my view, there are three main criteria for evaluating foreign policy:

(1) Security. Government should protect Americans against — and reduce the risk of — attack by any foreign nation or by terrorists.

(2) Personal liberty. Government must provide security without undermining the rights of Americans.

(3) Prosperity. (a) Taxes and government spending for military purposes should be minimized. (b) Government should not

interfere with peaceful trade between Americans and people in other countries.

NEUTRALITY: NON-INTERVENTION

The first element in libertarian foreign policy is neutrality — or, as some put it, non-intervention. The U.S. government is not the ruler of the world. It has no authority to act as a government (militarily, economically, or otherwise) past the borders of the United States. The globe is covered with governments of sovereign nations, each having authority over its own area.

But U.S. policy makers have long acted as if they have the right to go anywhere and do anything. Reverse the situation and see how dangerous this idea is. If some Iraqis were traveling in America and were arrested for breaking the law in Chicago, and if Iraqi soldiers invaded Chicago to rescue them, Americans would be outraged. We would declare this an act of war and call for serious reprisals against Iraq. Such a response would be understandable.

The same principle applies in reverse. The U.S. government's interventions in other countries are unjustified. Predictably, such interventions increase the risk of drawing our nation into war and jeopardizing our security. Intervention generates hostility toward the U.S. government and individual Americans. It raises the risk that Americans outside U.S. borders will be killed or taken hostage by terrorists. The 9/11 attack by Islamic terrorists is just the most recent example of this tragic, but predictable, pattern.

THE DISASTER OF INTERVENTION

The U.S. government's long-standing interventionist policies have been a security disaster. The worst part is the waste of young Americans lives.

The pattern of U.S. military intervention is typically as follows. Somewhere in the world, different factions get into a dispute. Often the existing government is one of the factions and the worst offender. The U.S. government intervenes to assist one faction, and dispatches U.S. military personnel. Young Americans die.

Other people die. Eventually, politicians' concern about the "crisis" wanes, the public loses interest, or the American death toll mounts to embarrassing levels. The U.S. military pulls out and things return to how they were before. Vietnam and Lebanon are perfect examples.

Consider also the Persian Gulf War in 1991. One Arab country (Iraq) invaded another (Kuwait). The U.S. military stepped in, killing over 100,000 Iraqi soldiers and civilians. Fortunately, very few Americans died. The U.S. military departed from Iraq, but U.S. troops were deployed in adjacent countries. Saddam Hussein remained in power in Iraq. (That is, until the United States decided 11 years later to attack him again; see below.)

The events in Yugoslavia from 1992-1994 were similar. Factions with centuries-old ethnic and religious disputes were engaged in so-called "ethnic cleansing" — more accurately described as mass murder. The U.S. military bombed the country. That action, intended to protect one faction (ethnic Albanians), resulted in more deaths and the rapid departure of ethnic Albanians from the Kosovo province. Later, that faction returned to Kosovo and the other faction (Serbs) fled for their lives. U.S. politicians patted themselves on the back for this foreign policy "success."

As deplorable as ethnic strife is, the United States can do little to improve the situation if people in foreign nations are not willing to settle their own disputes and negotiate their own peace agreements. Using the U.S. military as peacekeeper results in an expensive and risky long-term presence that, at best, temporarily suppresses the violence. Tension usually flares and the killing resumes as soon as American troops leave.

It is also worth noting that the U.S. government has ignored many conflicts (similar to that in Yugoslavia) in places like Sierra Leone, Afghanistan, Rwanda, Sudan, Turkey, Indonesia, and Sri Lanka. Politicians apparently believe they have some unique insight to pick and choose which foreign humanitarian tragedies "require" U.S. military involvement. Sadly, these politicians never provide a believable rationale to explain why intervention is justified in one foreign hellhole but not another.

Finally, American taxpayers bear the exorbitant cost of trying to save the world — one bloody conflict at a time — with U.S. tanks, guns, and bombs. Taxpayers then continue to pay the price, often for years, as U.S. troops settle in to protect an unstable peace and to support the remaining "approved" faction in a conflict that was never any of our nation's business to begin with.

IRAQ AGAIN

Our federal government never seems to learn. After the terrorist attack on the World Trade Center and the Pentagon on September 11, 2001, Americans naturally wanted to retaliate against the aggressors. The target was Al-Qaeda and its leader, Osama bin Laden. President George W. Bush chose to invade Afghanistan without a formal declaration of war from Congress.

Ironically, the Taliban, which held power in Afghanistan where most of Al-Qaeda's camps were located, had been supported and supplied by the U.S. government in the 1980s when they were fighting Soviet invaders. Now, they became the enemy. The Taliban were removed from power, but American troops remained there, engaged in a continual low-level war against a stubborn Afghani resistance. Osama bin Laden remained at large and Al-Qaeda continued its operations around the globe.

Frustrated by events, President Bush decided to invade Iraq and topple Saddam Hussein. The alleged justification for doing so was weapons of mass destruction (WMD) that Hussein possessed. It was also argued that Saddam was involved with Al-Qaeda in connection with the World Trade Center attacks.

Neither claim was true. There were no reasonable grounds to believe so, but the administration sold the story to a gullible American public. In 2003, the invasion was on, again without a formal declaration of war by Congress. It was supposed to be a short war, leading off with "shock and awe," and the Iraqis were expected to welcome the American soldiers as liberators.

Neither happened. The U.S. military did easily destroy Saddam's military and capture him. But that quick "victory" soon degenerated into a vicious and bloody guerilla war between Iraqi insurgents and the American soldiers who occupied their nation. Approximately 135,000 American troops remained in Iraq to battle that insurgency.

By mid-2005, the American death toll was over 1,700, with another 15,000 wounded. The Iraqis have suffered as many as 100,000 dead, mostly civilians. Although elections to create a new Iraqi government were held in January 2005, the U.S. military continued to suffer attacks on its troops. Iraqis who cooperated with the United States were also targeted. At this point, observers fear that an all-out civil war may explode among Sunnis, Shiites, and Kurds.

The U.S. attempt to export democracy by force to Iraq appears doomed. America's choice is to stay for decades, at the cost of billions of taxpayer dollars per month, plus the inevitable loss of life, or to cut its losses and leave the Iraqis to solve their own problems. My advice: leave now.

LIBERTARIANS OPPOSE ISOLATIONISM, SUPPORT FREE TRADE AND TRAVEL

Some people mistakenly confuse neutrality and non-intervention with "isolationism." Nothing could be further from the truth. Libertarians want to bring Americans and people in other countries together. Libertarians would halt U.S. military meddling in the affairs of others. An end to U.S. military intervention would promote increased harmony, cooperation, and friendship between Americans and the people of other nations.

Libertarians also want to remove legal obstacles to trade and travel. Libertarian free-trade policies would eliminate the barriers to productive human interaction across international borders. With such freedom, cultural exchanges, tourism, and commerce would flourish. That's the furthest thing from isolationism.

Finally, Americans should never be prohibited from voluntarily helping people in other countries. Americans should be able to go themselves, or send money, food, medicine, or weapons — at their own expense — to help those in need or under threat. An example is the American Jewish community's voluntary aid to Israel. Such individual "foreign aid" is more focused and far less wasteful than the politically motivated foreign aid doled out by U.S. politicians.

THE RIGHT TO FREE TRADE: PEACE AND ABUNDANCE

Libertarians advocate free trade for several reasons. Individuals have the right to engage in commercial transactions with each other on any peaceful, voluntary, and honest basis. It does not matter whether those engaging in economic activity live in different cities, different states, or different countries. As human beings, each of us has the right to offer goods and services to willing buyers.

Free trade promotes international peace. Any time a trade barrier is removed, increased trade follows and the people who trade improve their conditions. When people in different countries trade with each other, they benefit in many ways. The last thing they want is a war to interrupt their trade. Interestingly, the U.S. government has never gone to war with another government while free-trade relationships existed between them.

History shows us that governments tend to follow the lead of other governments regarding trade barriers. If one lowers trade barriers, others tend to respond in kind. If one raises trade barriers, others retaliate. If we want other governments to reduce their trade barriers, the most practical policy is immediate removal of all U.S. trade barriers (tariffs, quotas, etc.). Removing trade restrictions is the single best way to improve the prosperity of Americans and others.

A capable defense for any country depends upon a productive economy to finance that defense. As other countries become more prosperous through increased trade with Americans, they will be better able to defend themselves. Further, as prosperity and friendly relationships with Americans improve due to increased trade and the development of market economies, the appeal of socialism (and other ideologies that scorn freedom) is reduced. So, too, is the likelihood of belligerence.

Consider Fidel Castro's Cuba. Since 1962, the U.S. government has imposed an embargo on trade and travel between the U.S. and Cuba. The embargo does not truly hurt Castro, because other countries have not joined in it. (Besides, despots rarely suffer even when their people starve. Despite widespread poverty in Cuba,

Castro has a personal fortune of $550 million, according to *Forbes* magazine.) However, the embargo does give Castro ammunition to propagandize the Cuban people into believing all their economic problems are caused by the U.S., rather than his failed socialist policies.

When Americans and American goods are allowed into other countries, people want more of what America has: individual liberty, a market economy, and political freedom. It's amazing what messages blue jeans, video games, Hollywood movies, hip-hop music, and Big Macs carry. When allowed to see such products and to interact with the people who produce them, the oppressed subjects of totalitarian regimes quickly figure out that their lives would be better with free markets. The establishment of free-trade relationships with Cuba could very well spell a quick end to Castro's regime.

END MILITARY WELFARE

For decades, the U.S. government has stationed hundreds of thousands of military personnel in scores of foreign countries. In 2004, about 116,400 U.S. troops were in Western Europe, 37,500 in South Korea, and 47,000 in Japan. According to the Department of Defense, the United States had troops stationed in 135 countries in 2004.

With the war in Iraq and the broader "war on terrorism," the U.S. military budget is over $420 billion per year — and about 65% of it is for military expenditures outside the U.S. During the Cold War, the average taxpayer in West Germany or Japan paid less for the defense of his own country than the average taxpayer in America paid for the defense of Germany or Japan. This is "military welfare," pure and simple.

The long-suffering American taxpayer still partially finances the defense of wealthy countries in Europe, Asia, and the Persian Gulf. These countries are fully capable of deciding what military risks they face and what to do about it. They have the economic capability to pay for the military defense they need. They should act responsibly, make the decisions, and pay for them.

American military personnel should be brought home to defend Americans and our property here. That can be done with substantially reduced numbers and cost. A look at the world map — and a knowledge of military reality — demonstrates that there is no chance of a conventional military attack against the U.S. Any such attempt would surely and quickly fail.

NATO IS UNNECESSARY

The United States has been a member of the North Atlantic Treaty Organization (NATO) since shortly after the end of World War II. In the event of war involving European NATO countries, the U.S. agreed to come to their defense. During the Cold War, U.S. politicians said NATO was necessary to protect Western Europe from an invasion by the Soviet Union and its Eastern Bloc allies.

Although the Warsaw Pact — and any threat of invasion — is long gone, NATO lives on. Bizarrely, NATO has even begun inviting its former enemies to join. In 2004, the ex-communist nations of Bulgaria, Latvia, Estonia, Lithuania, Romania, Slovakia, and Slovenia joined the coalition. President Bush said the expansion would "refresh the spirit of this great democratic alliance" — but didn't explain why NATO was still necessary, given the lack of an enemy.

Obviously, there is no need for the U.S. to prepare for war in Europe. The European Union (EU) has more people (456 million versus 293 million) than the United States and a combined GDP that is equivalent (about $11 trillion). Europeans are more than capable of paying for their own defense.

While the U.S. has been withdrawing a significant number of troops from Europe over the past several years, it is time to complete the job. The U.S. government should immediately give notice that it is withdrawing from NATO, and continue the orderly return of all its military personnel back to the United States.

PERSIAN GULF OIL

During the Cold War, it was argued that if the U.S. were to withdraw from foreign military commitments, the Soviets would immediately "fill the vacuum." This argument was frequently used to justify the U.S. military presence in the Middle East where, it was said, we needed to keep Arab oil flowing to the United States. Even today, many argue that the United States has a "vital national interest" in Persian Gulf oil supplies. That contention was clearly behind the first Gulf War in 1991 when Iraq invaded Kuwait, and some argue that it played a similar role in the 2003 U.S. invasion of Iraq.

The argument that the U.S. must protect Persian Gulf oil supplies does not withstand scrutiny. Any aggressor country capturing Kuwait's, Saudi Arabia's, or any other Persian Gulf country's oil fields would do so *to profit from the oil.* Whoever controls the oil fields will produce oil and sell it. No government or dictator (however belligerent) would be able to resist the temptation to reap billions of dollars in profit by selling oil on the open market. That's why so many Arab nations — even ones that dislike the U.S. government for its support for Israel or the invasion of Iraq — continue to sell oil to Americans. They are as dependent on oil profits as the United States is on oil. In addition, there is too much competition in the international oil market for any one supplier to harm the U.S. by refusing to sell us oil.

In a free market, when the supply of any commodity is interrupted, prices rise. This tells other suppliers to increase production. It tells consumers to conserve and look for alternatives. Suppliers and entrepreneurs work harder to satisfy demand — and invariably come up with better and more efficient ways to do it.

When government interferes, and doesn't allow the market to work, those market corrections are delayed. An example was during the 1970s, when the government tried to allocate the distribution of oil and ration the sale of gasoline. The result was long lines at the pumps and higher prices. When such controls were lifted, the lines disappeared and prices eventually fell.

In short, getting the military out of the business of "protecting oil supplies" — and keeping the government out of the business of trying to micromanage its sale and distribution — would, in the long run, cost Americans less in lives, tax dollars, and energy prices.

A MILITARY LIMITED TO DEFENDING AMERICA

The Pentagon and Congress invariably seek expanded roles for the military. As the old saying goes, "When the only tool you have is a hammer, every problem looks like a nail." So it is with the military. With the vast might of U.S. forces at their disposal, politicians find endless reasons to use it. Several presidents have used alleged foreign threats to distract the citizens from domestic problems. Military personnel have been deployed to Central and South America to fight the War on Drugs. U.S. soldiers were dispatched to Somalia to help distribute food. Over the years, U.S. forces were sent to Morocco to supervise a civil war cease-fire, to Cambodia to clear land mines, and to Ecuador and Peru to monitor a disputed border region. They were deployed to Europe to keep peace in Bosnia and Kosovo. They battle Afghani and Iraqi insurgents daily. The result in almost all these cases was death and destruction — at great cost to the American taxpayers.

The primary legitimate function of the U.S. government is to provide security for Americans from the risk of attack by foreign powers. American defense should provide security for the American people in America. Libertarians advocate that the U.S. government adopt a policy of neutrality toward all other governments and withdraw from all military alliances. We should also terminate any commitments by the U.S. government to take military action on behalf of other governments.

U.S. surface naval forces should be returned from their deployments around the world to American coastal areas. The U.S. naval buildup is designed to enable the U.S. to engage in two wars concurrently around the world. That doctrine should end, and the U.S. Navy should focus only on defending the U.S.

Unless we Americans say, "Stop," there will be no end to U.S. military intervention abroad. We must demand that our military forces be used only to defend Americans and their property in America, and nothing else.

THE "WAR ON TERROR"

War is an evil whose costs are invariably overlooked or minimized — or even lied about — by the governments who engage in war. For politicians and military leaders, war is an opportunity to gain more power and status for themselves, while the people serve as cannon fodder, pay the bills, and make all the sacrifices. As Randolph Bourne said, "War is the health of the state."

Politicians frequently seek to label government projects a "war." Consider the War on Drugs, the War on Poverty, and the War on Crime. Politicians do so because government grows during wartime — and citizens tend to do what they are told in the name of patriotism. When the war is over, history shows that government never returns to its pre-war size and rarely relinquishes the power it seized.

President George W. Bush has played this age-old game by labeling his foreign adventurism a "War on Terror." Most frightening, he tells us that it is a war with no foreseeable end. If so, American military personnel will continue to die, Iraqis and other Middle Easterners will continue to be killed, Americans will continue to pay higher taxes, and Americans' personal liberties will continue to wither under government power-grabs like the PATRIOT Act — without end.

Terror is not a country against which the U.S. can declare war. Acts of terror are committed by individuals or groups who may or may not have connections with a government. (Many don't.) And despite being described by politicians as mere "madmen," terrorists almost always have a specific agenda. For the radical Islamists, it is primarily to get Westerners — who they see as "infidels" — out of Islamic lands. In other words, out of the Middle East, and particularly Saudi Arabia, the home of Mecca, Islam's most holy city.

Remarkably to those in the West, many terrorists are suicide bombers, willing to die for their cause. A recent investigation of 300 young Muslims, caught and interrogated by Saudi intelligence on their way to Iraq to be suicide bombers, indicated that very few had prior contact with any terrorist organization. The invasion of Iraq in 2003 led to their decision to die to "defend Islam." Thus, more U.S. interventionism breeds more enemies.

What if President Bush were to declare the "liberation" of Iraq over, and announce that all American military personnel in the Middle East would quickly return to America? What if he said that American companies and individuals could continue to travel to the Middle East — but would do so at their own risk? First, such a policy would save many lives and taxpayer dollars. Second, it would substantially reduce the risk of Islamic terrorist acts in America. Without Iraq as a flash point, groups like Al-Qaeda would find it more difficult to recruit the next generation of terrorists. (A U.S. policy of non-interventionism around the globe would reduce the threat even further.)

As you consider this, also consider the actual extent of the risk of terrorism in America. The 9/11 attack took 3,000 lives. It was clearly a monstrous and evil act which can never be excused. But plain old murderers in America killed 12,000 people in 2001. The same year 101,000 died in accidents, and flu and pneumonia killed 62,000. Bottom line: you have the tiniest fraction of a chance of being a terrorist victim compared to other potential causes of death. I'm not in any way minimizing the visceral horror of 9/11, or the personal tragedy endured by the friends and families of the victims. But the loss of liberty we have suffered at the hands of our own government in the name of "anti-terrorism" security (e.g., the PATRIOT Act) is clearly overkill in light of the real danger that terrorism poses.

A libertarian non-interventionist foreign policy cannot create a 100% peaceful, Utopian world. Nothing can. But it does have the *best* chance of reducing the future risk of terrorism in America. We should bring the troops home. Then, we should allow law enforcement and the intelligence community to do their jobs — so that terrorists planning to commit crimes on American soil can be identified and neutralized.

NUCLEAR ARMS POLICY

After World War II, the U.S. and the Soviet Union conducted a costly nuclear arms race, building nuclear arsenals able to destroy the entire world several times. With the worldwide collapse of communism, beginning in 1989 with the fall of the Berlin Wall, the collapse of the Warsaw Pact, and the political disintegration of the Soviet Union itself, the Cold War and the nuclear arms race have ended. Still, about 25,000 nuclear weapons exist in the possession of the U.S., Russia and a few other nations. The U.S. and Russia hold 95% of them.

The Russian nuclear arsenal is about equal to that of the United States. Since the Soviet Union dissolved, nuclear disarmament has moved rapidly. The Strategic Arms Reduction Treaty (START) was signed by Russia and the U.S. in 1991. In 2002, the U.S. and Russia signed the Strategic Offensive Reduction Treaty (SORT). Under these treaties, by the end of the year 2007, each country will have no more than 3,500 nuclear warheads and no more than 2,000 by the end of the year 2012. Those are positive steps in the right direction.

However, we can do more. The U.S. strategic nuclear arsenal has three types of missiles: land-based, submarine-carried, and bomber-carried. Any one of the three could destroy all humanity. We could eliminate 90% of the U.S. arsenal and still effectively retaliate against any country or group foolish enough to attack.

STRATEGIC DEFENSE INITIATIVE ("SDI")

In 1983, then-president Ronald Reagan initiated the development of space-based anti-missile systems, the Strategic Defense Initiative (SDI). The argument then made in favor of SDI was that it would provide a truly "defensive" system to replace retaliation with weapons of mass destruction as a deterrent to attack.

Several arguments have been made against SDI. Nuclear bombs can be made small enough to smuggle into the U.S. by small boat or pick-up truck. The expense to develop and build SDI would be huge. Some scientists contend that developing such a system is technologically impossible, at least for decades. However, during 1999, the U.S. was successful with a test of a defensive missile intercepting an offensive missile, giving reason to believe that the technological barriers could eventually be overcome.

A mutual desire for peace has replaced the tensions among former Cold War adversaries. It is obviously time to re-evaluate SDI now that there is no risk of a first strike from the Soviet Union. There is also another approach that could be taken with an SDI system: continue to develop it, but don't use the typical, wasteful military procurement methods. Instead, require defense contractors to bear the development costs. When they produce a working anti-missile system, they will get paid. Such an approach would encourage defense contractors to build the system only if there was a realistic chance of making it work at a relatively low cost.

NUCLEAR ARMS REDUCTION AND SDI

In light of current circumstances, I advocate the following policies regarding nuclear weapons and defense against possible attack:

1. Adopt an unequivocal "no-first-use" policy on nuclear weapons and negotiate with other countries having nuclear weapons for mutual no-first-use treaties.

2. Eliminate all land-based missiles in the United States and all bomber-carried nuclear bombs. Instead, rely for deterrence on submarine-carried missiles. One thousand submarine-carried nuclear missiles are more than sufficient. This would remove land-based missiles in America as potential targets.

3. Cancel further development and production of nuclear weapons and delivery systems.

4. Undertake development of SDI — or an equivalent anti-ballistic missile system — by offering the opportunity to defense contractors to bid on the project. The lowest bid for delivery of an *actually working system* will be accepted, and payment will be made upon delivery and proof of operation.

5. Pursue a treaty with all nuclear powers to dismantle all tactical (short-range) nuclear weapons.

6. Continue negotiations with Russia toward further mutual nuclear arms reductions.

With libertarian policies of neutrality, conventional military withdrawal from around the world, free trade, nuclear arms reduction, and no more Cold War, we can comfortably conclude that there would be minimal risk of a nuclear attack. There is some risk that existing nuclear weapons will fall into the hands of extremists. However, that risk is not one that requires the U.S. to maintain a nuclear arsenal of thousands of warheads. Free trade, non-intervention, and international diplomacy are better tools for reducing the risk of any rogue use of nuclear weaponry.

ADVANTAGES OF LIBERTARIAN POLICIES

Now let us reconsider the libertarian foreign policy of neutrality, non-intervention, nuclear arms reduction, and free trade. Consider its effects on the security of Americans, the effects on the personal liberties of Americans, and the effects on the economic well-being of Americans.

Under libertarian policies, American security would increase. First, because such policies would reduce tensions between the U.S., our former Cold War enemies, Third-World governments, and Arab nations. Second, increased trade would promote friendly relations between Americans and people in other countries.

In the area of personal liberties, we would eliminate conscription and the threat of draft registration. Further, we could reduce intrusive government surveillance of Americans in the name of national security. Finally, Americans would have more freedom to travel and engage in peaceful trade with people from other countries.

The prosperity of Americans would improve. Lower military spending would mean lower taxes. Approximately two-thirds of the current military budget is spent abroad. Rather than $420 billion per year in taxes for our current interventionist policies, we would pay a fraction of that for an effective national defense. The money currently spent on the military would flow into productive commercial enterprises, further lifting the economy. America's prosperity would also increase due to improved international trade relationships.

War may be, as Randolph Bourne said, "the health of the state." But *peace* is the health — and prosperity and security — of ordinary citizens. A libertarian policy of non-intervention, neutrality, and free trade would make that a reality.

CHAPTER EIGHT

TAXATION AS THEFT

> *To lay with one hand the power of the government on the property of the citizen and with the other to bestow it upon favored individuals to aid private enterprises and build up private fortunes is none the less a robbery because it is done under the forms of law and is called taxation.* — United States Supreme Court, Savings and Loan Association v. Topeka

Libertarians hold that people in government must abide by the same moral standards that apply to all people. Some federal government functions are legitimate, such as providing national defense and protecting the constitutional rights of individuals. A completely different question has to do with moral or immoral methods of financing these functions.

The traditional method of financing government is called "taxation." Taxes are as old as the institution of the state. In his book, *The State*, Franz Oppenheimer showed that the institution we call the state arose from tribal conquests and the exaction of tribute from the conquered people. Invariably one tribe or group would conquer another and require the conquered people to pay in crops, labor, or other property on a continuing basis. In return, the conquerors protected the conquered people from other marauding tribes. This "protection money" came to be called taxation.

The state and taxation have existed together throughout history. Wars are fought primarily to establish and maintain control over territory in order to extract taxes from its people. Some people produce wealth and are taxed, while others (ruling classes, the government) seize those taxes for their own benefit. It has always been so, regardless of the political system involved.

Americans revolted against Britain in 1776 largely because of oppressive taxation. To the colonists, liberty meant freedom from burdensome taxes. They held this view because of their knowledge of Europe, where they had seen the destructiveness of arbitrary and excessive taxes.

Libertarians call taxation by its accurate name: "theft." Taxation is simply some people using force to steal the earnings or property of other people. The taxpayer is threatened with fines or jail if he refuses to pay. If the taxpayer resists the government's thievery, officials have the power (not the moral right) to crush the resistance with whatever force is necessary, including lethal force.

DOES IMMORAL THEFT BECOME MORAL TAXATION BECAUSE THE GANG GETS LARGER?

Here's a way of thinking about taxes that you've probably never considered. If a man with a gun came to your home and told you to hand over a portion of your weekly earnings or be shot, you would consider that a violation of your rights. You would properly label it "armed robbery." If the same man came with 10, or 100, or 1,000 accomplices, your opinion would probably not change.

If the robber told you he intended to do good things with the money, such as defending you from other robbers, or educating children, or feeding the poor, you would justifiably not accept these rationalizations as proper reasons to rob you. Regardless of what a thief plans to do with the loot, theft is immoral. It cannot be condoned in a just society.

If you accept that premise, libertarians ask: How does theft become acceptable when the government is the one demanding your money?

Just because a group of legislators assert that, because they "passed a law" you must submit to their thievery, and just because they have men with guns at their command to compel you to submit, the immoral nature of taxation does not change. The underlying facts and principles remain the same, even though the process is obscured by politics, legalisms, and tradition.

An important libertarian goal is to show that taxation is based on *coercion*. We want to encourage people of good will to join in our efforts to eliminate coercive taxation as the method for financing proper government functions. Alternatives *do* exist for financing government — alternatives that are based on *voluntary* cooperation and respect for the rights of individuals.

INTERIM MEASURES: ELIMINATE CRIMINAL PENALTIES; PUT BURDEN ON TAX COLLECTORS

It is telling that government must enforce its tax code with criminal penalties. Anyone who fails to file tax returns or pay taxes runs the risk of being sent to prison. A taxpayer, even one without assets, cannot file bankruptcy and discharge a tax liability in the way private debts are discharged.

By contrast, as private citizens, we cannot put our debtors in jail. We can only file lawsuits and collect after a trial and judgment. If our debtor is insolvent, he can file bankruptcy and eliminate his debts.

So the first interim step in reforming our tax laws is to make the government abide by the same legal standard that applies to all people. We should remove the threat of criminal penalties, and require tax collectors to use civil courts to collect tax debts, just as you and I must use those courts to collect debts. Tax collectors should also assume the burden of proof. Currently, the law places the burden on the taxpayer to prove that the government is wrong about a tax bill. Let's even the scales — and make the government *prove* that an individual really owes money.

THE FEDERAL INCOME TAX

The Sixteenth Amendment to the U.S. Constitution was adopted in 1913, making it possible (according to questionable Supreme Court decisions) for the U.S. government to directly tax the income of the citizens. The modern income tax first entered our law in 1914, with the highest tax rate of 7% on the nation's wealthiest citizens.

During the debates in Congress, some argued that, since there was no upper limit on the proposed tax, it might go as high as 10% of a person's income. They were hooted down as alarmists, yet income tax rates went as high as 91% during World War II for people in the highest income bracket.

In 1943, the U.S. Supreme Court held that there is no constitutional impediment to stop Congress from imposing an income tax of 100%. Astonishingly, the justices said that leaving the citizens with *any* portion of their earnings is merely a matter of "legislative grace." As James Bovard, author of *Lost Rights,* wrote: "This statement, quoted hundreds of times in subsequent decisions in various federal courts, confirms that Congress has acquired an unlimited right to any citizen's income simply by a legislative decree. 'Grace' means 'favor.' That you are allowed to keep some of your income is simply a *favor* that politicians choose to give." It's difficult to make the case that any tax system that can seize 100% of your income is moral.

SURVIVE WITHOUT THE INCOME TAX?

Is it possible for Americans to survive without the income tax? There is every reason to believe we could. Remember, there was no permanent federal income tax before 1914. Without an income tax, the people of America prospered. By 1900, Americans were first in the world in per-capita wealth and standard of living.

Since 1914, and especially since World War II, the federal government has grown enormously and the federal income tax has risen to astronomical proportions. Most of that growth has occurred in the last 25 years. Since 1980, the federal budget has gone from less than $600 billion per year to $2.4 trillion per year.

Even if the income tax were not eliminated immediately, it could be substantially reduced. The federal income tax raises about 43% of the total amount of money that the federal government spends. Since high tax rates discourage productivity and low tax rates encourage it, the best policy is to cut income tax rates dramatically.

But that only takes us part of the way. It is also necessary to cut the level of activity (spending) of the federal government. By confining the federal government to its legitimate functions of national defense and the protection of constitutional rights, we could *repeal* the federal income tax. Then, we could eliminate that despised federal agency, the Internal Revenue Service.

LOW FLAT RATES OR NATIONAL SALES TAX AS AN INTERIM STEP

Drastic cuts in the income tax — or the total elimination of it — were, until recently, ideas considered too unrealistic for discussion in polite company. Today, establishment politicians are proposing an income tax at a "flat rate" in the 20% range, eliminating all graduated tax brackets. Others propose eliminating the income tax and replacing it with a national retail sales tax of 23%. Either of these proposals would be a considerable improvement. Both would reduce snooping and harassment by the IRS, cut down on our horrendous paperwork burden, and slash the costs of tax law compliance for individuals and business.

But these proposals by establishment politicians are not enough, since they merely maintain the high-tax status quo. In addition, Congress would never adopt them. Politicians are just too enamored with the power the current complicated tax code gives them to micromanage the activities of private citizens and to dispense financial favors to friends and special-interest groups.

Some libertarians have called for (as an interim step on the way to the goal of zero taxation) either a flat-rate income tax of 5% or a national retail sales tax of 5%. Further, most libertarians couple these proposals for real, substantial tax reduction with a call for reducing the federal government to one-third its current size (or less). In the final analysis, it is government *spending* that must be reduced so that tax reductions are made easier.

SOME ALTERNATIVES TO THE INCOME TAX

If people weren't forced to support government, would they do it? If so, how?

The current federal budget is approximately $2.4 trillion. Of that total, military spending will account for about $500 billion, depending on the final costs of U.S. military involvement in Iraq and Afghanistan. If the federal government were limited to providing national defense (as opposed to military adventurism in foreign lands) and protection of constitutional rights, federal expenditures could be less than one-quarter what they are now. So the amount of voluntary financing necessary would be a small fraction of the current budget we pay for with taxation and deficits.

Further, the Institute for Policy Innovation estimates that the taxation process itself costs $200 billion per year. Vast sums of money are paid to accountants, lawyers, and tax-return preparers who claim to understand the tax code. Americans spend millions of tax-preparation software and on tax-related record-keeping. As many as three billion man-hours are squandered annually by employees to comply with tax laws and by individuals who take time off from productive work to "do their taxes." The increase in wealth when that burden is lifted would make much more voluntary funding available.

There are many possible methods for voluntary financing of the legitimate functions of the federal government. According to the Giving USA Foundation, private charitable, educational, and other voluntary organizations in America raise about $250 billion per year. They raise additional billions in volunteer time from people who willingly support their efforts. We can learn from the voluntary fundraising methods these groups use.

Most people agree that national defense and protection of constitutional rights are important, and most people would voluntarily support them. However, most people are also understandably reluctant to support many of the other wasteful and unnecessary things the U.S. government does. This is why so many people object to paying taxes.

NATIONAL DEFENSE ENDOWMENT

One proposal for voluntary financing is to create a "national defense endowment." The U.S. government owns one-third of the land in America. It owns many other valuable assets — the

Tennessee Valley Authority, power plants, Amtrak, the Post Office, gold and silver bullion, oil reserves, and so on — which are not needed for the government's legitimate purposes. Portions of these assets could be sold off to raise the necessary sums to set up a national defense endowment fund.

The endowment, with prudent management, could invest in stock of publicly held companies or mutual funds, just as pension administrators invest funds. The income produced would provide ongoing national defense funding. Of course, all citizens would be encouraged to contribute voluntarily to the national defense endowment once it was established.

Americans have always rallied to defend their nation in time of genuine threat. Wouldn't they continue to do so — even if that national defense was funded by an endowment?

WAR DAMAGE INSURANCE

Another possibility is war damage insurance. Assume that insurance companies would write insurance to cover the risk of death, injury, or property damage resulting from an attack on the U.S. When insurance companies cover risks, they also often take steps to reduce the possibility of having to pay off on that risk. For instance, fire insurance companies do research on fire prevention methods, write building safety codes, and inspect private and commercial occupancies. It's all part of their sensible program to reduce the amount they might have to pay policy holders for fire loss.

If insurance companies wrote "war damage" policies, isn't it likely they would work to establish an effective national defense against attack? Or work to improve the prospects for peace?

Such activities might include funding research for the development of defensive technology, subsidizing military training, and financing intelligence gathering operations against potentially belligerent nations. They might also develop programs to improve international relations. An insurance-based national defense may sound strange at first — but it's just a logical step beyond what insurance companies already do to protect American's health, life, and property.

NATIONAL DEFENSE LOTTERY

Many state governments operate lotteries to raise money to pay for specific projects such as schools. The best thing about lotteries is that they are *voluntary*, not coercive like taxes.

Thus, a "National Defense Lottery" is one more possibility for voluntary financing. Would it work? That would depend on the willingness of you and other Americans to support it. Individuals could play the lottery because they hope to win large sums of money, or because they wish to contribute generously to defending their nation.

Again, a National Defense Lottery may strike you as far-fetched when you first consider it. But it is one more example of how libertarians are willing to "think outside the box" in an effort to liberate Americans from the onerous burden of taxes.

THE RIGHT GOAL

The foregoing suggestions are not intended as a complete list of possibilities. They do illustrate that it is possible to develop voluntary methods of financing proper government functions. They demonstrate that there *are* alternatives to taxation.

The important point is that we, as compassionate and rational human beings, should recognize that coercive taxation is immoral. There are better ways to fund government.

Therefore, our goal should be to replace the coercive method with voluntary methods that are more consistent with proper moral behavior. We may or may not be completely successful in reaching that goal, but it is the *right* goal.

CHAPTER NINE

EDUCATION: STATE CONTROL OR FREEDOM OF CHOICE?

Nothing is more important than giving young people opportunities to develop their minds and to learn about the world. All children, from the youngest age, are eager to learn. They constantly seek intellectual stimulation. The question is: What will they learn, from whom, and in what circumstances? More important are these questions: Who gets to decide? Will it be parents and students, or government bureaucrats?

Most adult Americans attended public — that is, *government-operated* — schools. Most American children now attend public schools. Unfortunately, there is a great deal of fault to find with the government-operated schools, both on moral grounds and on the basis of poor results. It is no coincidence that the operation of the public schools is morally bankrupt and the results deplorable.

STATE-RUN EDUCATION IS BASED ON COERCION

Libertarians seek to eliminate coercion in human relationships. As with any product or service, the relationship in education is between suppliers and consumers. On one side are suppliers: administrators, teachers, custodians, textbook publishers, etc. On the other side are the consumers: parents, children, and taxpayers. But this most definitely is not a peaceful, voluntary marketplace.

Government schools run on coercion. First: compulsory attendance laws. It is a crime if parents fail to deliver their children to school.

Second: compulsory financing through taxation. Compulsory attendance and compulsory financing together establish a near-monopoly. Like all protected monopoly businesses, government schools are inefficient, expensive, and relatively unconcerned about the welfare of consumers. Most customers can't afford not to use government schools — despite the low quality — because they're paying for them, and parents can't afford to pay taxes for public schools *and* tuition for private schools. Other taxpayers must pay for government schools even if they don't use them, or else they risk going to jail.

Third: coercion regarding subjects taught in the public schools. This explains the never-ending battles over prayer in school, sex education, creationism versus evolution, "inappropriate" books, and textbook content. Current textbooks tend to be a bland hodgepodge because textbook editors and school authorities try to satisfy, or not offend, a variety of competing interest groups.

Fourth: coercion regarding who can teach. Only certain persons with certain educational backgrounds are legally allowed to teach. In many states, school authorities harass parents who prefer to teach their children at home. The same thing sometimes happens to people who offer religious schooling. A few years ago in Nebraska, for example, seven fathers were jailed for contempt of court for educating their children in a church school. The children scored *higher* on standard tests than equivalent public school students and were willing to be tested regularly. The parents' only crime was refusing to obtain the state's permission to operate the school. State school authorities seem less interested in educational quality than in confirming their own power.

Fortunately, advocates of school choice and homeschooling have engaged in lobbying efforts and lawsuits that have gradually increased the power of parents to choose the type of education they think best for their children.

GOALS OF STATE SCHOOLS

Before state schooling began in this country, literacy rates were much higher than today. Regent University Professor William F. Cox, Jr. noted that, according to an 1800 study commissioned by Vice President Thomas Jefferson: "Most young Americans... can read, write, and cipher. Not more than four in a thousand are unable to write legibly — even neatly..." America's second president, John Adams, wrote: "A native in America, especially of New England, who cannot read and write is as rare a phenomenon as a comet." Despite that success, by the nineteenth century, professional educators began to promote the idea of state schooling, primarily to insulate themselves from parental control. They were not much concerned about literacy, since that was already happening with private education. A second motive was to homogenize the population, using state schools to remold immigrants — many of whom were Catholics from Ireland and Italy — into obedient citizens who would adopt the dominant Protestant ethnic group's values.

Nineteenth century advocates of state schooling did not attempt to hide their agenda. They argued that children were essentially the property of the state. They contended that the school's function was to indoctrinate children into patriotic, obedient citizens whose first loyalty was to the government — and that the main obstacle to achieving that goal was interference from parents.

The state-run school system has largely succeeded in achieving its goal of molding generations of unquestioning servants to the state. It is equally clear that intellectual literacy, on all subjects, has declined in those same schools.

SEPARATION OF EDUCATION AND STATE

There is no proper role for government in education. The founders of this country made one of the most valuable contributions to a peaceful and free society when, in the First Amendment to the U.S. Constitution, they established the principle of separation of church and state. They were aware of centuries of religious war and persecution resulting from political attempts to establish state religions and to suppress dissenting views.

The right to freedom in the area of intellectual development and personal philosophy is fully as important as freedom of religion — and for the same reasons.

Accordingly, a free society must have a separation of *education* and state — just as there is a separation of church and state.

DISASTER OF STATE SCHOOLS

Over the past 30 years, average per-pupil expenditures for public elementary and secondary schools have nearly doubled, rising from $3,931 in 1971-72 to $7,524 in 2001-02, in constant dollars. At the same time, class sizes became smaller, student performance declined, and violence increased. Today, nearly one out of four young people who graduates from or drops out of high school is a functional illiterate. Colleges and universities find that incoming freshmen need remedial training in reading, writing, and critical analysis. Children of poor and minority parents suffer most. Illiteracy in inner-city schools is as high as 40%. As a result, increasing numbers of adults cannot read or write. Citing U.S. Department of Education statistics in her 1998 book, *Human Resources,* Diane Arthur reports: "One in every seven American adults is a functional illiterate, unable to read, write, calculate, or solve even simple problems," and another "47 million adults are borderline illiterates."

The average private school tuition, according to a 2003 Cato Institute study, is $4,689, only two-thirds that of public schools — yet private schools educate better. In fact, a 1999 survey by the Public Agenda research organization found that Americans agree, 52% to 19%, that private schools "generally provide a better education" than public schools. In public schools, the level of violence and drug abuse is considerably higher than at private schools. Even public school teachers understand the advantages of private schools. The Institute for Justice reported that while only 11.5% of U.S. schoolchildren attend private school, 46% of public school teachers in Chicago send their children to private schools.

TAX CREDITS WILL BRING COMPETITION TO EDUCATION

As an interim measure (so long as the federal income tax exists), I advocate tax credits for anyone who pays for the education of any student. Educational tax credits will bring competition into education. A tax credit against federal income taxes would mean a one dollar reduction in tax liability for every one dollar paid for education.

I propose a $4,000 per year, per student, tax credit for any person, or any company, who pays for the education of any student, or any number of students. The tax credit would apply regardless of whether the student attended public or private school. We could also improve the effectiveness of the tax credit by changing state and local law to allow students to transfer to the school of their choice.

The tax credit should not be limited to parents. Wealthy individuals or corporations could provide "scholarships" to as many students as they want, and reduce their taxes by the amount of the scholarships. The tax credit should also be available for parents who teach their children at home.

With such a tax credit, parents, wealthy individuals, and companies could provide educational scholarships to students at virtually no out-of-pocket cost. It would also save taxpayers money because each student educated on a $4,000 tax credit in a private school saves the approximately $8,000 cost to taxpayers of public school funding.

Using the educational tax credit, many students would probably move from government schools to private education. This could not happen overnight, of course. Educational entrepreneurs would need time to get new schools launched or to expand existing schools. Meanwhile, government schools would scramble to become more efficient, cut costs, and be more responsive to the desires of parents and students. This is as it should be. In an open, competitive marketplace, those who do the best job of satisfying consumer demand survive and profit.

Open educational competition would also mean greater variety in subjects, systems, and methods to meet the desires of a broad spectrum of parents and students. The best teachers would be in great demand and their earnings would increase.

Libertarians have advocated educational tax credits, or similar education "vouchers," for many years. Now mainstream politicians are also calling for "choice" in education. Some public school districts allow students to attend any school, rather than making them go to the school closest to home. Milwaukee, Wisconsin has adopted a limited voucher system that allows students to decide which school to attend, and that school gets the tax money for that student.

In 2002, the Supreme Court upheld a Cleveland school choice program. (Supporters of the educational status quo had tried to argue that the program was unconstitutional because some parents used the vouchers to send their children to parochial schools.) Clint Bolick, of the Institute for Justice, predicted that the decision would help establish the legal principle "that parents, not bureaucrats, have the right to make essential decisions regarding their children's education." Let us hope his prediction is accurate.

BENEFITS FOR THOSE WHO NEED IT MOST

Poor and minority children would benefit most from expanded educational opportunities. The inner-city public schools, attended primarily by poor and minority children, are the worst. Tax credits will create private funding for poor children, allowing them to search out the best educational bargain. Today, only the wealthy can afford to send their children to private schools while also bearing the tax burden for state-run schools.

Oddly, when libertarians make proposals to improve educational opportunity by increasing freedom of choice, many people object. They contend that, if free to do so, some people might not send their children to school, causing those children to grow up ignorant. Or they say that some poor people could not afford education for their children.

Such objections ignore current reality. The present system produces a high amount of failure, frustration, ignorance, and illiteracy. Poor and minority children are the primary victims. Compulsory attendance laws only require *attendance* — not learning. Many kids are so frustrated by their experience in public schools that they not only do not learn themselves, they disrupt the learning process for others.

Many poor parents already make tremendous sacrifices to escape public schools and get their children into private schools. Some outstanding educational results are occurring in private schools in minority communities, such as the Marcus Garvey school in Los Angeles. A 2000 study by the Heritage Foundation found that Marcus Garvey students "routinely score two or more years above grade level in core subjects."

Remember, too, that the educational tax credit proposal is not limited to parents; it will also allow wealthy individuals and businesses to support education for poor students. An additional benefit will be to break down barriers between rich and poor. Poor parents seeking better education for their children and wealthy individual and corporate taxpayers seeking tax benefits will naturally come together, building bridges of cooperation between classes and races.

BUSINESSMEN GIVE POOR KIDS A CHANCE

Not willing to wait for government to act, in 1998 the late John Walton (WalMart heir) and Ted Forstmann (Forstmann Little & Co.) created, with their own money, the Children's Scholarship Fund, which provides partial tuition assistance for low-income families to send their children to private schools. Currently, more than 23,000 children are using CSF scholarships. These children are attending private school not only due to the generosity of CSF donors, but also because of the sacrifices made by the families themselves, who pay about 50% of their children's tuition. The Fund focuses on elementary education because the earlier a child receives sound schooling, the better. Scholarships are awarded to all eligible children in a family to attend the school of their choice.

The response from families was staggering. For the first scholarships in 1999, the parents of nearly 1.25 million eligible children from over 20,000 communities applied. Scholarship winners were selected in a random drawing. The response to this program is an amazing demonstration of the dissatisfaction with government schools — and of the willingness of poor parents to sacrifice so their kids can get a quality education. We can only hope that other wealthy individuals and corporations will follow in the footsteps of John Walton and Ted Forstmann, as this is a truly libertarian way to get government out of education. By their example, they demonstrate that government schools are what many parents are forced to *settle for* — not what they would freely choose.

CONCLUSION

Any program that gives greater choice to parents and students is an improvement over the current government monopoly on education. The tax credit proposal is preferable to school "vouchers" because voucher programs require a continuing role for government bureaucracy to administer them. With tax credits, the individual simply makes the choice and reflects payments to schools on his or her tax return.

However, increased choice for students among public schools, vouchers, or tax credits represent only small improvements. They are merely the first steps toward the goal of complete separation of education and state.

Finally, let us never forget: Utopia is not an option.

Our options are an educational system based on coercion — or genuine educational freedom of choice. For anyone with any honest concern and compassion for the young and their mental development, freedom of choice in education is the only answer.

CHAPTER TEN

PROHIBITION REVISITED: THE INSANITY OF THE WAR ON DRUGS

> *Now what I contend is that my body is my*
> *own, at least I have always so regarded it. If I*
> *do harm through my experimenting with it, it*
> *is I who suffers, not the state.* — Mark Twain

The use of alcoholic beverages is as old as recorded history. Invariably, some people have sought to prevent others from producing, buying, selling, or consuming alcoholic beverages. One example was the period referred to as "Prohibition" in America from 1920 to 1933. The Prohibition experience is instructive because it shows so clearly the disastrous results of attempting to suppress peaceful activity with criminal law.

Possession of an alcoholic beverage does not violate the rights of any other person. To grow the grapes or grain from which liquor is made does not violate anyone's rights. To produce alcoholic beverages in a peaceful and honest manner violates no one's rights. Nor does drinking, buying or selling the liquor violate the rights of any other person.

Similarly, there is no justification for imposing criminal penalties on anyone who produces, buys, sells, possesses, or uses *any* intoxicating substance. People own themselves and have the right to control their own lives, bodies, and honestly acquired property. People have the right to deal with each other in whatever peaceful and honest manner they choose. This includes the production, use, and trade of alcohol, marijuana, cocaine, or heroin.

Please note: Libertarians do *not* recommend the use of drugs. We contend only that individual rights must be respected, and that it is wrong to put people into prison or otherwise punish them for exercising their rights in any peaceful way. Libertarians also argue that the consequences of drug prohibition are far more destructive than the drugs themselves.

INEVITABLE BAD CONSEQUENCES OF PROHIBITION AND CRIMINAL PENALTIES

What happens when peaceful activities are made crimes? The experience of Prohibition is a classic example and a lesson for today. The "War on Drugs" is simply a more vicious and destructive replay of the failed experiment of alcohol Prohibition.

1. The law does not work.

People who want to engage in a peaceful and honest activity will do it regardless of the law. Prohibition did not effectively prevent anyone from drinking. Today's drug laws do not prevent people from purchasing drugs. Similarly, gun control laws do not prevent anyone from having a gun. Anti-gambling laws don't stop gambling.

2. Making criminals out of peaceful people ruins their lives.

Alcohol Prohibition instantly made America a nation of criminals. Alcohol had been legal since long before America's founding. But Prohibition made the production and sale of alcohol a crime — and millions of drinkers were suddenly engaging in criminal acts and consorting with criminals to do what had previously been perfectly legal and respectable.

In the same way, current laws against the use and sale of drugs make criminals out of millions of peaceful Americans who threaten no one. People labeled as criminals, and introduced to a black market, may be willing to engage in other criminal activity. Productive citizens may have their lives destroyed by arrests.

3. The price of the illegal commodity is much higher than it would be in a competitive market.

The law of supply and demand works in illegal as well as legal markets. Making a substance illegal reduces the supply, and the shortage causes higher prices. Heroin, for example, is not inherently an expensive drug; produced legally, it costs scarcely more than aspirin. However, sold illegally on the black market, the cost of heroin soars by perhaps 50 times that. So an addict's daily heroin needs can cost $100 or more. This huge difference in price is due solely to the law. Such high black-market prices have devastating consequences, as we shall see.

4. Huge black-market drug profits encourage violent criminal profiteers.

Because of the high profits to be made in illegal markets, those risk-takers most willing to engage in crime go into these illegal markets. The most ruthless and violent criminals are those who succeed in black markets. Prohibition spawned organized crime in America. Organized crime continues to exist today, supported by illegal markets in drugs (and in other prohibited consensual activities such as prostitution and gambling). In essence, the War on Drugs is a price-support system for organized crime.

5. High black-market prices encourage crime and destroy lives.

Alcoholics and tobacco addicts can easily pay for their drugs of choice with mere pocket change, because they are legal. Thus one almost never hears of alcoholics or smokers committing crimes to obtain money to pay for their addictions. Those addicted to illegal drugs, however, must pay enormous black-market prices for their drugs. Many cannot pay those prices with the wages earned by legal jobs. Some therefore turn to crime: robbery, prostitution, drug selling, etc. In this way, the Drug War encourages billions of dollars of property crime and destroys lives by driving people into the criminal underworld.

Ironically, those who advocate strong drug laws typically argue that such laws are needed to suppress crime associated with drug use. But this argument has cause and effect exactly reversed. The crime associated with illegal drugs is largely caused by the criminal law that makes them illegal. Very little crime has to do with drugs per se; it is caused by the War on Drugs itself.

6. The existence of illegal markets corrupts the criminal justice system.

To protect their huge profits, criminal suppliers bribe police, courts, and jailers. Some police become drug dealers themselves or steal money and contraband from the illegal dealers or the evidence lockers. A sick, symbiotic relationship develops between lawmen and drug dealers. Recent criminal prosecutions of law enforcement officers show a pattern of beatings, filing false police reports, lying in search warrant affidavits, planting evidence on suspects, stealing money, and resale of drugs stolen from dealers. According to the Drug Policy Alliance, "Approximately half of all police officers convicted as a result of FBI-led corruption cases between 1993 and 1997 were convicted for drug-related offenses."

Former Seattle chief of police Norm Stamper is angry about what the War on Drugs is doing to his profession:

> "Almost all of the major police corruption scandals of the last several decades have had their roots in drug enforcement. There isn't an unscathed police department in the country. New York, Los Angeles, Chicago, Philadelphia, Detroit, Washington, D.C., Memphis, Miami, Oakland, Dallas, Kansas City — all have recently suffered stunning police drug scandals. You won't find a single major city in the country that has not fired or arrested at least one of its own for some drug-related offense in the past few years..." (From *Breaking Rank: A Top Cop's Exposé of the Dark Side of American Policing,* Norm Stamper, 2005.)

It is revealing that drug users inside prisons have no problem getting illegal drugs. This not only indicates widespread corruption, it proves the futility of the entire Drug War: if drugs can't be kept out of maximum-security prisons, how can they possibly be kept out of an entire nation?

7. Law enforcement becomes more expensive for the taxpayer and misdirected as well.

By some estimates, over one-half of the tax dollars spent for law enforcement and the criminal justice system is spent on the suppression of peaceful consensual activities, i.e., on "victimless crimes," chief among them drug crimes. The courts and prisons are so clogged with drug dealing or possession cases that judges must free perpetrators of violent crimes. In 2003 the FBI reports there were 755,186 arrests for marijuana alone — far more than the 597,026 arrests that same year *for all violent crimes combined.* And 88% of those marijuana arrests were for mere possession. According to the National Organization for the Reform of Marijuana Laws (NORML), since 1992 over six million Americans have been arrested on marijuana charges.

Because of the War on Drugs, the United States now imprisons more of its citizens than any other nation in the world. More than 2.1 million U.S. citizens — one out of every 138 Americans — are behind bars, according to an April 2005 report by the U.S. Bureau of Justice Statistics. The U.S. incarceration rate — 726 people per 100,000 — is the highest in the world. (By comparison, Britain has 142 people per 100,000 in prison; China: 118; France: 91; Japan: 58.) The numbers continue to rise yearly. Most of this is due to low-level drug offenses, or crimes otherwise related to the Drug War.

All this gravely endangers our safety, regardless of whether we use drugs. Police busy investigating and arresting alleged drug users are not available to fight *real* crimes — like rape, robbery, and murder.

8. The products in illegal markets are of a lower quality than in legal markets, thus endangering consumers.

During alcohol Prohibition, people sometimes died from impurities in contraband liquor. Thousands went blind or suffered other serious ailments. "Bathtub Gin" was the name given to this dangerous impure booze. Today, the millions of Americans who consume illegal drugs are similarly at risk; most drug deaths and illnesses are due to impurities or inaccurate dosages from drugs, not the drugs themselves. And this is directly due to the Drug War. In illegal markets, consumers can't know what they're buying, and they have no legal protection against fraud, shoddy products, or violence committed against them by dealers. In legal markets, by contrast, organizations and publications such as *Consumer Reports* provide reliable information about products and services, and the legal system is there to protect your rights.

9. The War on Drugs causes illness, suffering, and death.

As mentioned, relatively few deaths occur from straight drug use, and none at all from marijuana. Most so-called "drug-related deaths" are actually the result of impurities and unknown substances mixed in the drugs, uncertain dosages, and the violence associated with drug dealing. The high cost of drugs, due to their illegality, leads addicts to neglect their health and to engage in dangerous activities, causing further sickness and death. The Drug War drives many good people, who have become addicted to drugs, into a dangerous underground world of crime, disease, and death.

AIDS is a major health concern, and the government spends a great deal of money on research to combat it and to control its spread. Yet state laws, encouraged by the federal government, outlaw hypodermic needles without a prescription. This leads to the dangerous practice of needle sharing. AIDS spreads rapidly among intravenous drug users who share needles. Hepatitis and other diseases similarly spread in this manner.

Further, the War on Drugs has become a barbaric war against the sick and the dying. Marijuana can be extremely helpful in the treatment of many illnesses; for example, it can help cancer victims respond better during radiation treatments and help AIDS sufferers maintain their appetite. Heroin is particularly effective in pain management for cancer victims and other sufferers. Yet the drug laws deprive sick people of these beneficial treatments. Adding to this misery, the War on Drugs has terrified many physicians into drastically under-prescribing pain medication for patients suffering from severe chronic pain.

10. Competition in illegal markets is based on violence as opposed to peaceful, honest trade.

Alcohol Prohibition was known for its violent gang wars over territories. The Drug War is the same. Frequently, innocent victims get caught in the crossfire. Gang warfare on the streets is a sad and vicious fact of life in many big cities. Noble Prize-winning economist Milton Friedman estimated that several thousand homicides per year in the U.S. occur because of drug prohibition. Economist Jeffrey A. Miron argues that ending drug prohibition would likely cut the U.S. homicide rate by as much as 75%.

11. The War on Drugs is destroying civil liberties.

Enforcers turn to entrapment, tax laws, and violation of the citizens' constitutional protection against unlawful and unreasonable search and seizure. Police harass peaceful citizens on the highways, the high seas, and at the border. Everyone's financial privacy suffers in the search for drug money. We all face having to submit to periodic urine tests and roadblocks. Police can stop and search you if you fit a vague "profile" of drug couriers. Recent court decisions have, in effect, created a "drug law exception" to your constitutional protection against unreasonable search and seizure. Even America's long-standing tradition of prohibiting military enforcement of civilian law has been seriously eroded: the armed services are now routinely used against American citizens in the Drug War.

12. All your property may be taken, merely upon police accusation.

Under asset forfeiture laws, the police can seize money or property without due process of law, merely by claiming it had some connection with illegal drugs or dealing. These laws undermine traditional constitutional protection. The police do not have to prove you committed a crime or even accuse you. If the police claim your money or property was somehow connected with a drug deal, they can seize it and you must prove your innocence to recover it. Many people carrying large amounts of cash have been victimized by these laws; the assumption is that only drug dealers have any reason to carry cash. Victims often have no money left to hire a lawyer. Perversely, the laws allow police departments to keep the seized money or property — so police have a strong incentive to make false accusations, seize the loot, and then hope the victim is unable to prove his property was free of drug taint.

13. The Drug War is racist.

The War on Drugs is waged disproportionately against minority Americans, and mostly in poor neighborhoods. According to the Drug Policy Alliance, minorities don't use or sell drugs at significantly higher rates than whites. Blacks constitute 12.2% of the population, and only 13% of all drug users. Yet blacks account for 35% of those arrested for drug possession, 55% of persons convicted, and 74% of people sent to prison. Blacks are stopped, searched, arrested, prosecuted, and incarcerated at far greater rates than whites, and typically sentenced to far longer prison terms.

Black men are sent to prison on drug charges at 13.4 times the rate of white men.

Nationwide, one in three young African-American men are incarcerated, or on probation or parole. The Drug War is the major culprit in these figures. The stigma of criminal conviction, in turn, severely hampers educational and job prospects. In short, the Drug War is destroying a generation of young blacks, crushing them into an unskilled, poverty-stricken, politically powerless permanent urban underclass.

14. Relations with foreign countries suffer.

If the demand for contraband exists in the U.S., foreigners will find ways to supply it. Our government then puts pressure on foreign governments to crack down on their citizens. Ultimately, U.S. agents and even the U.S. military may begin operations in those countries to smash drug suppliers, as has happened in many countries. Innocent civilians are injured and killed, and people naturally resent U.S. interference in their domestic affairs. These operations never halt the flow of drugs into the U.S. — drug sources are endless. But the people in those countries get one more reason to fear, resent, and hate the U.S. and its people.

15. Criminal drug laws encourage more dangerous drugs and experimentation.

The Drug War doesn't keep drugs out of the country. It only increases the price of the substances and thus encourages more trafficking, as well as the development of alternative — and ever-more-dangerous — drugs. Drug producers have a great incentive to develop and sell more powerful drugs, which are less bulky and easier to smuggle. Ironically, because of this, less-dangerous drugs are frequently replaced with more dangerous ones. During alcohol Prohibition, bootleggers replaced beer and wine with hard liquor; today, marijuana becomes hashish, and powdered cocaine is concentrated into crack cocaine.

The risk to users is obvious. As law enforcement drives consumers away from well-known drugs with predictable effects, venturesome drug consumers take greater risks with their minds and bodies by trying untested and more potent substances.

DRUG USE AND DRUG LAW HISTORY

America's tradition in drugs is one of individual choice and individual responsibility. Before 1914, there was virtually no federal limitation on, nor regulation of, drug use and sale. Opium and its derivatives were freely available in a variety of forms, as was marijuana. Yet we had no significant criminal problems or social problems associated with these substances. Many people regularly used drugs, including opium and cocaine, and led normal productive lives, just as millions of people today live normal lives while using legal drugs like alcohol and caffeine.

In 1914, the Harrison Narcotics Act, the grandfather of today's drug laws, was passed, and the lives of millions of peaceful drug users suddenly became nightmares, as the federal government began arresting and persecuting them. Even the doctors who tried to treat addicts were arrested and imprisoned by the thousands.

Marijuana was outlawed by the federal government in the 1930s, thanks to an outrageous propaganda campaign of lies and absurd distortions (see the film *Reefer Madness* for typical examples). That campaign was led in part by ex-Prohibition agents who, some argue, were looking for another Prohibition-type war in order to protect their jobs. Many of those same absurd arguments from the 1930s are still used today to justify the war against marijuana. Yet no one has ever died from an overdose of marijuana, and it has far less serious health effects than legal drugs like alcohol and tobacco.

WHAT IF THE DRUG LAWS WERE REPEALED?

If the laws against drugs were repealed, would Americans all become drug addicts? Would our society go down the drain? There is no reason to think so. This frequently asked question is based on several major fallacies. First, it assumes that people cannot currently get illegal drugs. But today, anyone who wants illegal drugs can get them, quite easily.

The questions also assumes that illegal drugs are invariably the most dangerous and addictive. Yet tobacco and alcohol are addictive, cause severe health problems, and many more deaths than all illegal drugs combined. Still, tobacco and alcohol are sold across America. In part, that's because we as a society recognize that the consequences of outlawing these substances would be far worse than keeping them legal. Around 50,000 people die each year from alcohol poisoning; more than 400,000 deaths each year are attributed to tobacco smoking. In contrast, no one has ever died from marijuana overdose.

Then there is the example of Prohibition's repeal. Alcohol consumption did increase, but only slightly. There was no noticeable increase in alcoholism or other social problems.

Since 1973, 12 states — Alaska, California, Colorado, Maine, Minnesota, Mississippi, Nebraska, Nevada, New York, North Carolina, Ohio, and Oregon — have significantly decriminalized marijuana possession for personal use, generally removing the threat of jail time. Several major studies have found no significant increase in marijuana use or other social problems in those states. Indeed, the National Academy of Sciences, Institute of Medicine wrote in 1999: "There is little evidence that decriminalization of marijuana use necessarily leads to a substantial increase in marijuana use."

It's also worth noting that over the past 20 years Americans are also using less legal alcohol and tobacco, as a result of education and social pressure.

The European experience is also instructive. Holland follows a policy of tolerance for personal use of marijuana and hashish, allowing adults to purchase small amounts in coffeehouses. No violence or social problems accompany this practice; marijuana use there is half the rate of the United States. Britain's National Health Service allows doctors to prescribe heroin for severely addicted people. The result: many addicts emerge from nightmare lives of crime, prostitution, and shattered families, and resume normal and productive lives.

YOUNG PEOPLE AND DRUG LEGALIZATION

When discussing legalizing drugs, young people are a special concern. Legalization may well make drugs less attractive to young people by removing the aura of glamour and rebellion that illegality has given drugs. In the Netherlands, where marijuana is freely available for adults, a smaller percentage of adolescents use marijuana than in the U.S.

Legalization may also make it harder for young people to get drugs. In annual polls conducted by the National Center on Addiction and Substance Abuse, high school students regularly say that marijuana is easier for them to obtain than beer. The reason is simple: businesses fear the stigma and penalties of selling to minors. Drug dealers have no such concerns. We frequently hear about drug dealers on school campuses; people who sell alcoholic beverages rarely hang around schools trying to interest the students in liquor.

THE POSITIVE CONSEQUENCES

What positive consequences might we see from repeal of the drug laws in America?

1. Organized crime would lose tens of billions — perhaps hundreds of billions — of dollars per year in illegal drug profits.

2. The streets and our homes would be far safer because the illegal drug dealers would be gone and their violent turf wars ended. Drug transactions and use would occur non-violently in stores, bars, and homes.

3. Burglary, mugging, shoplifting, and car theft would plummet because addicts would no longer be paying astronomical prices for their drugs and could support their low-cost habits by working at normal jobs.

4. The street corner drug dealer would be gone. Children in poor and minority neighborhoods would no longer have that negative role model to lure them into drug dealing.

5. Police, courts, and jailers could turn their attention to ridding our communities of violent career criminals, and billions of law enforcement tax dollars (an estimated $33 billion at the federal level alone) would be saved. Courts and prisons would no longer be clogged. There would be plenty of room in existing jails and prisons for *real* criminals — those who commit crimes of violence or theft.

6. Thousands of peaceful people convicted of illegal drug possession could clear their names of the stigma of the criminal label and return to productive lives in society.

7. Illness and death from the use of adulterated drugs would plummet, as would the transmission of AIDS by intravenous drug users who would no longer need to share needles.

8. Drugs that are currently illegal would become available for beneficial medical treatment.

9. You would regain your right to privacy and your constitutional protection against unreasonable search and seizure by overzealous drug warriors. Your property would be safe from seizure without due process.

10. People with drug abuse problems would be more willing to ask for help, and those who want to help them would have more resources available for this important work.

11. More harmonious relationships could develop between Americans and people in other countries as U.S. military drug warriors ended their interventions in drug-supplying countries.

CONCLUSION

Adults have the right to control their own bodies. They have the right to decide for themselves what to eat, drink, smoke, or otherwise ingest. And they have the obligation to take responsibility for the consequences of their decisions. Making drug use a crime violates the rights of all peaceful people and is morally indefensible.

If we consider all the negative results of attempting to suppress peaceful activities with criminal laws, and if we compare those results to the positive results to be expected from repeal of such laws, any reasonable person should come to the same conclusion. Just as alcohol Prohibition was a disaster, so are criminal laws against drugs. Just as Americans finally repealed alcohol Prohibition, we must end the War on Drugs.

CHAPTER ELEVEN

SOCIAL INSECURITY

The debate about the future of the Social Security system continues to make headlines. And for good reason: the system is in big trouble. Since the late 1970s, Congress has tried numerous times to "reform" Social Security by increasing payroll taxes, raising the retirement age, taxing Social Security benefits, and limiting benefits. American workers are paying the cost of these futile efforts to save Social Security from collapse. Thirty-five years ago the program took $30 billion a year from workers. Now it takes about $658 billion , more than a quarter of total federal spending. Today (2005), the Social Security tax rate is 12.4% on the first $90,000 of your earnings each year. A vast majority of workers now pay more Social Security taxes than income tax. "Social Security" is a misnomer. It is not secure at all, and most people know it, especially young Americans.

Today, many older Americans think of the old-age benefits under Social Security as the primary source of their retirement. But even the Social Security Administration acknowledges that the program "was never meant to be the sole source of income in retirement." Unfortunately, the government has seriously misinformed the American people about Social Security, how it works and what it can do. We have been told that Social Security is some sort of insurance, investment, or pension plan. It is none of these things. People think they have "paid in to" Social Security. This is a mistake. The Social Security system is merely a government tax and redistribution program whereby working people are taxed and the money is immediately paid out to retired people. There is no pool of money that anyone "paid in to" which exists as a retirement or investment fund. Nor do Americans have any legal right to the money they paid into Social Security; the Supreme Court has ruled that politicians can change benefits levels or even abolish the program at will.

THE SOCIAL SECURITY SYSTEM IS INSOLVENT

The Social Security System is insolvent. We should view it the way we do a bankrupt corporation. The system has about $12.8 trillion in unfunded liabilities. This means that, under current estimates, all of the money which must be paid out in the future to those entitled to receive it — if the system continues unchanged — would equal $12.8 trillion. The only way to raise the money to pay it is to increase taxes on working people in the future. It is estimated that it would take a 50% increase in Social Security taxes to continue to fund current benefit levels. As the Cato Institute's Michael Tanner notes, "That's a terrible burden to impose on our children and grandchildren."

Right now, the government is collecting more in Social Security taxes than the amount of benefits being paid out because the "baby boom" generation workers are now in their prime productive years. But the government is not accumulating that surplus and investing it for the future; every penny is spent immediately on other government programs. In turn, the government issues IOUs in the form of special Treasury bonds that are placed in a so-called Social Security "Trust Fund." But the trust fund is a scam. As President Bill Clinton's fiscal year 2000 budget explained, trust fund assets are not "real economic assets." Instead, the bonds are "claims on the Treasury that, when redeemed, will have to be financed by raising taxes, borrowing from the public, or reducing benefits or other expenditures." Meanwhile, 78 million baby boomers are approaching retirement themselves.

OUR AGING SOCIETY

Our society is growing older. When Social Security began in the 1930s, average life expectancy was less than 65, the age people began receiving benefits. So most workers were not expected to receive *anything.* The government actually expected to make money on running the system.

It's great that we all live longer today. But because our parents and grandparents still begin to receive benefits at age 65, the Social

Security system will inevitably drown us all in red ink.

When the system began, there were 16.5 working people paying into the system for every retired person receiving benefits. That ratio has been dropping steadily. Today there are 3.3 workers for every one retiree. By 2040, it is anticipated that it will fall to two to one. By then, the government will have only three choices to stop the fiscal hemorrhaging: slash benefits, significantly raise taxes, or borrow trillions of dollars. The system cannot survive under such circumstances. And everyone knows it. A January 2005 *USA Today* poll shows that two-thirds of those under 30 years old don't think Social Security will pay them *any* benefits when they retire.

Trying to continue on the same course will cause major conflict between young and old. It is increasingly apparent that benefits for the elderly under Social Security and related "entitlement" programs (e.g., Medicare) are among the largest factors in the explosive growth and cost of the federal government. Today, the federal government spends about $22,000 per year for each senior citizen for Social Security and Medicare. These two programs alone equal more than 7% of the gross national product. Younger working people will find ways to evade the system, just as many people now work in the "underground economy" to evade excessive taxation. Tax increases of the magnitude necessary would so depress the economy as to cause a massive recession or a complete economic collapse. Thus, rather than providing security, the existing Social Security system is a prescription for disaster and *loss* of security, not only for older people, but for everyone.

SYSTEM HURTS POOR COMMUNITIES

The Social Security system has had particularly deleterious effects on the poor and minorities. First, if they die before reaching the qualifying age of 65, they get nothing. If they survive long enough to receive anything, the benefits cease when they die. The poor die younger, and black males have the shortest life expectancy of all. So they get the *least* — while losing the highest portion of their income to the Social Security payroll tax. As Deroy Murdock noted for the National Center for Public Policy Research: "Social

Security essentially transfers money from working black men and women (who die earlier) to older white women who live the longest." By contrast, if African-Americans could keep the tax money taken for Social Security and invest it themselves, they would own the invested proceeds to fund their retirement. Upon death, it would go to their family.

Social Security is a lousy investment by comparison to private markets. For the average worker, the expected monthly Social Security benefit payment will be a fraction of what the same amount would pay if put in the most conservative investment vehicles. That is, if instead of paying the payroll tax, the worker put the same amount into the lowest-risk investments available in the market and then purchased a private annuity with the proceeds at age 65, the payments from the annuity would be approximately *four times* what the worker would receive in Social Security benefits.

Eighty percent of American workers pay more in payroll taxes for Social Security and Medicare than they do in income taxes. This hits poorer communities especially hard. Lower income workers have nothing left to invest or spend after paying the payroll taxes, so investment capital is being drained from those communities, which means it is not available for small business development. That in turn means fewer job opportunities for our poorest citizens.

STUMBLING TOWARD A SOLUTION

Even though it is widely recognized that Social Security cannot survive, politicians have always been leery of discussing the problem. Elderly voters are numerous and many are fearful of losing "their benefits." Politicians are fearful of telling the truth about the Social Security bankruptcy because it might cost them the next election.

By 2005, however, the political establishment could no longer deny the obvious — that Social Security was headed for economic disaster. President George W. Bush floated a proposal to offer voluntary personal savings accounts to younger workers. Under his plan, workers would have the option of putting up to 4% of their income into stock and bond funds instead of into the Social Security system.

Bush's plan was, at best, a halfway step. Workers over 55 could not participate; younger workers' retirement accounts would be managed by the government; and the federal government planned to borrow a trillion dollars so it could continue to make Social Security payments to retired workers. Instead of replacing a bankrupt program, Bush said his plan would merely "fix the Social Security system."

As timid as it was, Bush's plan represented a breakthrough, since it introduced the idea of private accounts into mainstream political debate. It also generated the expected backlash from senior citizen's lobbying groups and big-government politicians, who denied that Social Security was in crisis. All that is needed to "save" the program, they vowed, are minor tax hikes, or broadening the wage base on which the Social Security tax is paid, or slightly boosting the age of retirement by a year or two.

Meanwhile, other nations have been more forthright about addressing their looming retirement problems. One country that has substantially improved its situation is Chile. That country largely privatized its system by setting up 12 investment funds that are privately run, much like mutual funds here. Workers are required to invest a set percentage of their earnings in the approved investment funds and cannot remove it until retirement. This creates competition among the funds. Unlike the U.S. Social Security system, the invested money remains the property of the worker. The results have been quite beneficial for the Chilean economy. The savings rate is high, which provides a major source of capital for the expansion of business, which in turn has led to higher levels of employment. The workers are accumulating retirement funds, that they own, much more rapidly than before.

Although the Chilean government does not manage any of the investment funds, it does regulate them; nor may the workers opt out of the system. It is compulsory. The political circumstances could change and result in greater government involvement, although that appears unlikely at this time. All things considered, moving from the current bankrupt U.S. system to a semi-private system like that pioneered by Chile — which is several steps beyond what President Bush proposed — would be an improvement, although lacking the complete freedom libertarians advocate. In addition to Chile, more than 30 other countries, including Britain, Sweden, and Australia, have established some kind of personal accounts for workers.

California also provides another model for reform. Its Public Employee Retirement System (CALPERS) is the pension fund for government employees. Its members can opt out of Social Security. By investing in securities, the fund managers provide pensioners a much higher return on their contributions than what they would receive from Social Security.

A TOUGH SOLUTION FOR A TOUGH PROBLEM

So how can we avoid our coming Social Security disaster? The solution begins by facing up to the hard realities. Unlike President Bush, libertarians understand that the current system cannot be fixed. Minor tinkering, partial privatization, and more federal debt will not provide a long-term solution. We must recognize that we are dealing with a bankruptcy situation — and the best we can hope for is to end the problem and cut our losses. There is no "fair" way or perfect solution.

The following proposal is designed to solve the problem quickly and in the least-burdensome way, but does not claim to be perfect. Remember, Utopia is not one of the options.

Our purpose is to phase out the government's bankrupt Social Security system as quickly as possible. At the same time, we want to protect older citizens with more secure contractual investments and free all Americans from the crushing tax burdens that will otherwise bankrupt the entire country in time.

We begin with those people age 56 or older, including those 65 or older already receiving benefits. People in this 56 and older age group would receive 100% of the pay-out under the proposal. Those in the age group from 52 through 55 will receive a percentage of the proposed pay-out based on their age: 52 = 20%, 53 = 40%, 54 = 60%, 55 = 80%.

For each person in the total category (all those age 52 and older) it will be possible to do an actuarial analysis, much as an insurance company would do, to determine the present discounted value of the future Social Security benefits that person would receive if he or she lived to average life expectancy. In simple terms, this would be the amount of money one would need to invest at current interest rates in order to make the Social Security benefit payments to the average person after age 65. This gives us a lump sum figure for each person in the class.

Each such person would choose between taking the lump sum or purchasing a life insurance annuity contract from a private insurance company to replace the Social Security benefits they would have received under current benefit schedules.

FUNDING THE BUY-OUT

What is the source of the money to finance this Social Security buy-out? The system is bankrupt. So is the entire United States government. When dealing with a bankruptcy, the aim is to use the bankrupt entity's assets in order to pay its creditors at least some portion of what is owed.

The United States government holds a huge amount of assets which are not relevant to its legitimate purposes of national defense and protection of constitutional rights. In fact, the U.S. government owns one-third of the lands in the United States. It also owns a multitude of other very valuable assets such as the Tennessee Valley Authority, other power plants, motion picture studios, millions of vehicles, Amtrak, postal service assets, NASA, satellites, etc. Portions of those assets ought to be sold, in a fashion which will maximize the proceeds, to fund the Social Security buy-out. According to some estimates, the federal government owns more than $12 trillion in assets, more than enough to fund this proposed Social Security buy-out.

Finally, anyone entitled to receive payment under this proposal who did not actually need it would be encouraged to decline payment.

Another alternative for phasing out the government's bankrupt system is the simple "opt-out" plan. Simply give every citizen of working age, including retired persons, the option of having nothing to do with Social Security ever again (no payroll taxes, no benefits) as of an announced date. Most likely, the great majority of younger people would opt out and many retired people would stay on, except for the more wealthy who are receiving no benefits because of their other taxable income.

Of course, with fewer young workers paying into the system, the government would have less revenue with which to make payments to retired workers. So this opt-out plan would also have to be financed through the sale of government assets. Or, politicians could choose to fund remaining Social Security obligations by cutting other unnecessary government programs.

While such an opt-out plan would not solve the problem as quickly as an immediate buy-out plan, it would accomplish the same goal, since the system would likely die of attrition within a couple of decades.

LIFE WITHOUT SOCIAL SECURITY

Either proposal means the end of the government Social Security system entirely. Security will *increase* for the elderly who take their lump sum, to invest as they see fit, or who purchase a private annuity. Unlike government benefits, which can be altered or ended at the whim of Congress, private annuities are contracts with insurance companies that must be honored and are enforceable in court.

There would be no more Social Security tax that today takes 12.4% of every dollar you earn up to $90,000. All younger workers would be free of the increasing Social Security tax burden. Think of what you would do with that extra money. *Your* money, that you earned. The economy would receive a great boost because of the tax relief ($658 billion per year), the resulting increased private spending, and the jobs created to meet new consumer demand.

Perhaps most gratifying, we would avoid the impending economic collapse and the inevitable conflict between young and old that the current system will cause if we do not have the courage to change it. I'm confident that many older Americans will see the great benefit of freeing their children and grandchildren from the disaster in store for them if Social Security is not brought to its well-deserved end.

CHAPTER TWELVE

WHAT ABOUT THE POOR?

Our federal and state governments manage many programs that extract taxes from working people and, after absorbing a significant portion for bureaucratic overhead, distribute the money to people considered needy. Food stamps are one example, but there are many others: Medicare, housing subsidies, unemployment insurance, etc.

Millions of people are poor, unemployed, disabled, or otherwise unable to support themselves. Infants without parents, the mentally incompetent, very old people, and others are clearly not capable of providing their own care and support. Somehow, someone must help them. The question is not whether, but how *best*, to help.

To libertarians, the political issue is: What is the legitimate use of force? Government welfare programs are financed by taxation. Some people (those in government) use force to carry out programs by taking and spending the property of other people. It is instructive to compare the results of government programs to the results of private organizations that also provide assistance to people. Government welfare, based on coercion and bureaucracy, is generally acknowledged as a failure. Private charity, based on love and compassion, is hailed for its remarkable successes.

STEP ONE: DECRIMINALIZE WORK

Most people receiving welfare, or who are chronically unemployed, would prefer to support themselves by working rather than receive demeaning public assistance. The first step in helping the poor is to eliminate all governmental laws, regulations, restrictions, and obstacles to people who would be self-supporting if they had the opportunity. In other words, decriminalize work.

A perfect example of a counterproductive law is the "minimum wage law." In 1997, Congress increased the federal legal minimum wage to $5.15 per hour. (Some states have higher minimums.) In doing so, politicians made it a crime for one person to work for another for $5.14 an hour or less. This law clearly violates the rights of such people. The minimum wage law makes unemployable those whose current job skills are too low for a willing employer to hire them for $5.15 an hour. The fact that minimum wage laws destroy jobs is widely accepted. In his book, *Minimum Wage, Maximum Damage*, Jim Cox notes that during a 1989 debate over whether to raise the federal minimum wage to $3.85 or $4.25, the only argument was over how many people would lose their jobs — 300,000 or 600,000. "For perhaps the first time, it was readily admitted by all concerned that substantial job losses would occur whatever the amount of the increase," Cox wrote.

This "unemployment effect" falls most heavily on inexperienced, poorly educated, young people. With no skills or experience, many are unable to find employers willing to pay them $5.15 per hour, although many potential employers would be willing to take them on as lower-paid trainees. As trainees, they could acquire work experience at the first rung of the ladder and move up later. The minimum wage law bars them from getting that first job. As a result, many will be unemployed forever.

Congress knows the job-killing effect of the minimum wage law. Why don't they repeal it? The hidden purpose of the law is to protect organized labor. The unions deliver many more votes than younger, less organized people. Politicians simply count the votes and keep raising the minimum wage, even though it causes unemployment among the young and unskilled.

Some people argue that we need a high minimum wage to prevent employers from "exploiting" workers by paying them low wages. But most working people earn much *more* than the minimum wage. How could that be if employers grind down workers to the lowest possible wage? There is a great demand among employers for skilled workers. Because of this competition, skilled workers can demand and receive very good pay, much higher than the legal minimum.

Indeed, nearly all workers receiving minimum wage are the youngest beginners. Frequently they are students living at home, and many are part-time employees. Nor do they stay at minimum-wage jobs for long. Most move quickly on to higher-paid jobs. The argument that the minimum wage must be raised so workers can support a family does not square with reality. The only effect of the minimum wage law is to cause unemployment among the youngest, least experienced, most vulnerable job-seekers in our society.

LICENSING AND PERMIT OBSTACLES KILL JOBS

Licensing and permit restrictions prevent many people from going into a variety of occupations. The Interstate Commerce Commission (ICC), for instance, for years limited entry into the trucking business, as well as limiting where truckers could ship their goods or what they could carry. This reduced competition among trucking companies (and raised prices for consumers). It also had a serious racist effect, preventing black-owned businesses, in particular, from getting started.

The history of the Civil Aeronautics Board (CAB) shows how regulation hurts and deregulation helps. Economic regulation of the airlines by the CAB was the rule until Congress ended it in 1985. Before deregulation, not one new major airline was started. After deregulation, entrepreneurs created scores of new airlines — including Southwest, JetBlue, and AirTran — that expanded travel options for millions of Americans. Air fares plummeted. By 2002, the U.S. Department of Transportation estimated that passengers were saving $19.4 billion per year from deregulated fares. The new airlines also put people to work and revitalized smaller airports. Notably, the older, established companies invariably prefer regulation because it protects them from competition. Smaller, newer, independent companies oppose regulation because they want to offer their services to more people.

By contrast, consider the personal computer industry. Many millions worldwide work at producing and servicing hardware and software. The industry continues to grow rapidly, providing better products at continuously lower prices. It is almost completely unregulated by government. No reasonable person could believe that its progress would have been as spectacular if Congress had created, say, a Federal Computer Regulatory Agency in 1980. If that had happened you can be assured that you would never have seen Apple's groundbreaking Macintosh computer, the Google search engine, lightweight laptops, or Microsoft Windows XP.

Within states, regulatory bodies make it difficult for people to start businesses. Entry to hundreds of professions — e.g. taxi driver, hairdresser, plumber — is strictly limited by licensing. New York provides some provocative examples. Black hair styles include a unique type of African hair-braiding. But in order to legally work as a hair braider, New York City requires a license issued only after 900 hours in cosmetology school — *where nothing relevant to hair braiding is taught.* New York City allows only a specific number of taxis (exactly 12,187 as of 2005). A taxi license in New York City costs $400,000. Not many poor people can afford that. Transportation suffers. The demand for transportation that the government is incapable of satisfying is being met by illegal cabs and an underground "jitney" system. Rather than letting poorer entrepreneurs start small transportation services, the city has issued as many as 1,000 citations a month to stop them.

Libertarians would take a different approach. We would eliminate all legal obstacles to anyone offering goods or services. This provides opportunity for people who are poor — or just getting started — to offer services that no one else is providing because of the regulatory obstacles. And every new small business will put more people to work.

ZONING HURTS THE POOR

Zoning — and other laws making it a crime to work at home — should be repealed. The city of Houston, the fourth-largest city in the U.S., has no zoning. From time to time a proposal is put on the ballot in Houston to allow a vote on whether to institute zoning. Each time the voters reject it. The greatest vote against zoning in Houston always comes from the poorest part of the city. Poor people know that with zoning will come restrictions on their ability to work in their homes.

Consider the poor woman with children who offers to baby-sit for working mothers in her neighborhood. Before long, she will be visited by the zoning department, the health department, the building department, child welfare, the business license bureau, and who knows what else. She will be told that she is unqualified to care for children. The area is not zoned for it. Her home does not have the required number of bathrooms or fire escapes. Regulation kills solutions real people find for their own problems. Today, when affordable child care has become a major political issue, removing regulations that obstruct home child care is an obvious solution.

CUT TAXES AND REGULATIONS

The most effective way to create jobs is to reduce taxation and regulation of business. The higher the tax burden, the more difficult for business to open, expand, or survive. Regulation of business has the same effect. Surveys of small businesses show that the greatest obstacle for them to expand beyond one or two employees is additional paperwork and government red tape.

Businesses complain that heavy federal and state regulation destroys their ability to operate profitably. And no wonder. The Competitive Enterprise Institute's Clyde Wayne Crews estimates that federal regulations cost business and consumers $877 billion in 2004. So businesses close up shop, or move to states with slightly more hospitable regulatory climates, or move out of the country entirely.

Government adds to the problem by passing laws that require business to provide specific benefits to workers. The added costs of compliance eliminate jobs by causing businesses to remain small, rather than grow and take on more regulatory burdens. For example, the federal Occupational Safety and Health Act (OSHA) kicks in with 10 employees. The Americans with Disabilities Act (ADA) becomes effective with 15 employees. The Family and Medical Leave Act (FMLA) arrives with 50 employees. And there are many more. Any sensible business owner would try to avoid expanding if it meant crossing these expensive thresholds.

Remember, there is no free lunch. Regulations cost money and jobs. If a company must spend $50,000 to modify its building to accommodate wheelchairs, that $50,000 cannot be put into product development or worker salaries. The effect is the same when employers must give government-mandated benefits to employees. The cost of doing so means more benefits for those working — but fewer jobs for those looking for work. Further, all the regulatory officials, regulation writers, and inspectors receive salaries, paid from your tax dollars, for spending their time telling other people what to do rather than producing goods and services people want to buy.

Some argue that when companies work to satisfy the regulations, that creates jobs. Nonsense! Do hurricanes create jobs? After a hurricane, people do more work to clean up and rebuild, yet no one thinks frequent hurricanes (or wars or riots) would be good for the economy. Any reasonable person understands that the net effect of frequent destruction of economic resources is to reduce everyone's standard of living. Using valuable resources to satisfy coercive regulations rather than to satisfy voluntary consumer demand has the same effect.

STEP TWO: PRIVATIZE WELFARE

A better approach to providing assistance for the truly needy is to privatize welfare.

Massive government welfare programs, especially at the federal level, have been with us for decades. During that time the cost to the taxpayer has increased tremendously. The federal government spends about $312 billion of your taxes a year on welfare programs, according to the Heritage Foundation. Yet many of the officially designated poor, who receive government benefits, are doing pretty well. Forty-six percent of them own homes. (The average "poor" person's home has three bedrooms, one and a half baths, a garage, and a patio, according to the Census Bureau.) Most have a car, televisions, VCRs, microwave ovens, and air conditioning. In most respects, America's "poor" have a higher standard of living today than the average middle-class American family had in the 1970s.

This is not to say that there are no truly poor people. But it does raise questions about government welfare. If you take the official number of Americans living in poverty (37 million in 2004) and divide it by the amount of money the federal government spends annually on welfare programs (about $312 billion), you get a figure of $8,432 per person. If all the tax money taken for government welfare programs were simply divided up among the poor, each family of four would receive about $33,700 per year. Obviously, they do not receive such lavish benefits. The question is: who does? Government employees running the welfare programs receive a hefty portion of it. Government welfare is terribly inefficient and certainly does not guarantee that those truly in need are taken care of properly. Many slip through the cracks.

Compare government welfare programs and programs of assistance conducted by private organizations such as churches, temples, the United Way, the Salvation Army, the Red Cross, Goodwill Industries, etc. These private groups raise about $250 billion per year in donations — and untold billions more in volunteer time — from people willing to support their efforts voluntarily. They are also much more efficient, with their administrative overhead averaging only about 10%.

GOVERNMENT WELFARE HURTS US ALL

Government welfare programs actually cause harm. Since massive federal government welfare programs started in the 1960s, almost $9 trillion (in 2003 dollars) has been taken from taxpayers for these programs. The hundreds of billions of dollars per year in tax money taken from working people to pay for government welfare programs undercuts the economy. Removing that tax burden, so that individuals and companies could use their funds to expand their businesses or buy consumer goods, would give the economy a tremendous boost. Many of the people now on welfare could go back to work — something the great majority of them would prefer.

Government welfare programs insult and demean all of us. They tell us we have no compassion; that only legislators and bureaucrats have compassion. They tell us we don't know how to effectively help people. They tell us we are unwilling to provide assistance to the needy unless we are forced to do so. Not one of these premises is true.

Government welfare interferes with our ability to express compassion for our families, neighbors, and needy people everywhere. Because of the heavy taxes Americans pay, we have less money left over to use as we think best to help other people.

Libertarians believe we must respect the compassion that others have because it is the same compassion we experience within ourselves. Most people know government welfare programs are terribly inefficient but still continue to support them precisely because people *are* compassionate. People don't want to see others in distress. We all want to live in a world where people generously help each other. The fatal mistake is to believe that compassionate and effective charity can result when government force is used in the place of a genuinely charitable spirit.

Government welfare undermines natural human compassion. It seduces people into allowing "someone else" to take care of the problem. It becomes easier to put Grandma in an institution and let others (taxpayers) pay for it, rather than to provide help for Grandma at home.

Government welfare programs are demeaning. Social workers pry into the personal lives of welfare recipients because taxpayers are naturally and justifiably concerned about welfare fraud — about people who are not "entitled" under the welfare rules to receive assistance.

Government welfare creates a perverse motivation for welfare workers. That is, government workers perpetuate the system because they are its primary beneficiaries. We have created a "welfare plantation" — ever-growing and expanding — that has the effect of locking the poor in that condition. Charles Murray's *Losing Ground,* which examines the effects of major federal welfare programs since the 1960s, shows that the percentage of people classified as "poor" has remained remarkably stable even as the programs have grown larger and more costly. Government programs don't cure poverty; they perpetuate it. Welfare creates incentives for people to avoid work, capitalize on victimhood, and remain in a perpetual state of dependency.

In 1996, the federal government finally acknowledged this, and passed welfare reform legislation that put a five-year limit on assistance and required welfare recipients to find work. Unfortunately, the reform effort was half-hearted. Even as politicians put some limitations on welfare, they boosted spending on child care, funneled more welfare dollars to states, and left "69 major means-tested programs, including food stamps, housing, and Medicaid" largely unchanged, reported the Heritage Foundation.

Despite its limitations, the reform effort liberated hundreds of thousands of Americans from poverty and dependency. "Caseloads plummeted and poverty decreased — often dramatically — for every racial category and age, including children," noted Michael F. Cannon on NationalReview.com. So did federal spending on welfare decrease, too? Unfortunately, no. "Even with the historic reform in 1996, the welfare system is expensive and growing," the Heritage Foundation reported in 2004.

The lesson of the 1996 reform effort is clear: the government can't solve the problem of poverty, and politicians will never "reform" welfare out of existence.

POSITIVE EFFECTS OF PRIVATIZING WELFARE

The best thing we can do for the poor and disabled is to privatize welfare — to eliminate government welfare programs. Lower taxes will help private business expand and increase employment. More people working means fewer needing assistance. With lower taxes, working people will have more left in their paychecks and will be better able to contribute to assistance programs through churches, temples, and other charitable institutions.

What will happen to the welfare workers if government welfare ends? These government employees are typically highly skilled and well educated, many with college degrees. Their skills would be in great demand in a rejuvenated economy freed from the welfare tax burden. They should do quite well in that economic boom. Let us be compassionate and give them that opportunity.

With the privatization of welfare, more people will be able to do more to help the poor in the most effective ways possible, working with others to solve the real problems of real people in their communities. The most effective assistance can be provided to the truly needy and deserving. This will not create Utopia, of course, but the private way of providing assistance is clearly superior to expensive, demeaning, and counterproductive government welfare programs. As a practical matter, personal liberty and responsibility work best.

Finally, remember the moral issue. If you see someone you think needs help, you have three basic options. You can help that person yourself; you can try to persuade others to help; or you can use government to force others to help. To a libertarian, the first two options are morally commendable. The third is morally reprehensible.

CHAPTER THIRTEEN

ECONOMIC FREEDOM, PERSONAL FREEDOM

A libertarian discussion of the economy begins with a concern for the right of all persons to do what they desire with their own lives, bodies, and property. People engaged in business do not fall into some second-class category, with inferior rights, simply because they are working to make a living. People have the right to deal with each other in any peaceful, voluntary, and honest manner. This includes producing, selling, buying, and using all the varied commodities and services available in the marketplace.

Where the right of people to engage in peaceful and honest production and trade is recognized, the resulting economic system is called a "free market." This is a natural state of affairs. As one wag put it: "A free market is what happens when no one does anything to prevent it." Libertarians advocate the free market because it is the *only* system consistent with individual rights.

In comparison to any alternative, the free market has also proven to be the most productive economic system. What is the alternative? In a word, "statism" — which comes in three major varieties: fascism, communism, and socialism.

FASCISM, COMMUNISM, AND SOCIALISM

Fascism is a political-economic system in which people legally "own" property, but government officials make the important decisions about its use. Under fascism, government officials typically regulate wages and prices, decide which products may be produced, hand-pick who can operate companies, and determine who may work in which jobs. Italy during the World War II era is the classic example of a fascist nation.

Although the U.S. is most frequently referred to as a free-market nation, it has clearly had its fascist periods, such as during World War II. In the early 1940s, the U.S. government essentially ran the economy in the name of the "war effort." Federal bureaucrats imposed wage-and-price controls, prohibited the manufacture of many consumer goods, and required companies to build tanks, guns, and fighter planes.

Depending on the amount of government control over economic affairs, a system can degenerate from predominantly "market" to "fascist." Many respected observers today argue that the U.S. economy is more fascist than free market. They particularly point to the local level, where intrusive government regulations such as rent control, zoning, and growth controls limit the use of private property.

The political system in which government owns most of the major industries is called socialism. Sweden, Venezuela, and Tanzania are examples of socialist countries. While those nations do allow some free enterprise, their governments exercise extraordinary control over the economy via ownership of large companies, industrial planning, high taxes, and restrictive trade union laws.

When the government controls the *entire* economy (except, perhaps, for some tiny enterprises), it is called communism. All the significant decisions about production and distribution are made by government-controlled central planning boards. The former Soviet Union is the classic example of a communist system. Today, North Korea and Cuba are two of the remaining examples of this failed economic model.

LITTLE FREEDOM IN CONTROLLED ECONOMY

Under fascist or socialist systems, government officials usually restrict personal and political liberty. Individuals have limited choice in choosing careers, using their property to make a living, or making important decisions about the productive areas of their lives. Most significantly, such conditions make it very easy for government officials to stifle political dissent.

Governments that control the ownership and use of computers, printing presses, fax machines, the Internet, and broadcasting technology have the power to decide who is allowed to create and distribute newspapers, books, speeches, and essays. They have the power to control what is broadcast on radio and television. Dissenting views are prohibited. In North Korea, for example, radio and televisions "are pre-tuned to government stations," notes the BBC.

Personal liberty depends on economic liberty. Or, to think of it from the opposite point of view, consider Leon Trotsky's classic communist dictum: "Who does not obey shall not eat."

People around the world have thrown off communist and other authoritarian governments. Their common cry is for free elections (democracy) and free markets (a market economy). This is no coincidence. Control of the economy is the primary tool used by dictatorships to keep people poor, suppress dissent, and thwart any challenge to the ruling party elite.

FREE MARKETS MEAN HIGH PRODUCTIVITY

The free market depends on recognition of individual rights, particularly the right to property. In order to be productive, a person must be able to use the resources he owns, starting with his own body, in ways he believes will be most beneficial. A free market cannot function without legal protection of an individual's right to own and control his or her private property.

Why is the free market so productive? Because people always enter economic transactions believing that doing so will benefit *them*. Two individuals who decide to conduct business do so because each anticipates he will be better off as a result. For instance, if I offer to sell you my cow for $1,000 and you decide to buy, this means I have better uses for $1,000 than I do for a cow. You, in turn, have better uses for a cow than for $1,000. Each of us feels we will be more productive with what we are getting than with what we are giving up. According to our own best judgment, each of us will be better off than we were before.

Recognizing people's property rights — and leaving them alone to engage in peaceful and honest economic activity — increases productivity for *everybody*. A free market creates an expanding economic pie. When people know they'll retain the benefits of their efforts, they work harder, produce more, save more, and are more innovative. This explains why, since the beginning of the Industrial Revolution, in those parts of the world with greater economic freedom, the standard of living has increased for all. This occurs even as the population has grown. The economic pie becomes larger — and everyone gets a larger slice.

Where government interferes *least* in the economy, productivity increases more rapidly. In Hong Kong for instance, the British government intervened very little in the economic affairs of the people. As a result, this small island with no natural resources was able to support millions of people and grow wealthy. (How Hong Kong will fare now that control of it has reverted to Communist China remains to be seen.)

History provides a perfect laboratory example with East Germany and West Germany. After the devastation of World War II, Germany had to rebuild. East Germany was under communist rule, and government officials made every major economic decision. Meanwhile, West Germany established a relatively free economic system.

The result? Forty years later, West German workers had a per capita income at least 50% greater than that of East German workers and a much higher standard of living. West Germany productivity since World War II has been widely hailed as an economic "miracle." East Germany's centrally planned economic system, although subsidized by the Soviet Union, ultimately collapsed in 1989, along with most other communist economies.

CENTRAL PLANNING INEVITABLY FAILS

From the late 19th century until very recently, most intellectuals viewed socialism or communism as the "wave of the future." One of the giants of free-market economics, Ludwig von Mises, in 1922 published a book entitled *Socialism* in which he demonstrated why centrally planned economies cannot succeed.

Mises' argument was groundbreaking and brilliant. Without the pricing mechanism available only in a free-market economy, there is no guidance for government planners. The pricing mechanism is the free interplay between supply and demand that sets prices. Without it, planners can't judge the relative value of goods, services, and economic options. Do consumer want more apples or potatoes? Should factories produce more cars or trucks? Should a construction company hire ten workers to dig a ditch or use one mechanical backhoe? Should carpenters build houses or apartment buildings?

Without the guidance of rising and falling prices (and profits), central planners can only guess. There is no way for them to know how to best direct the production and distribution of resources. There is no way to know whether their decisions are good or bad. There is no way to know what consumers truly want (and are willing to pay for).

Unfortunately, not much attention was paid to Mises (or the other critics of socialism) until the collapse of communist economies in the former Soviet Union and Eastern Europe seven decades later finally proved him right.

Today, socialist economic theories have no credibility. All but a few deluded ideologues recognize that central planning can't work. The big issue in Eastern Europe and most of the former Soviet republics today is how best to move towards a market economy. In fact, many of the economists helping to lead their formerly socialist countries look for guidance in the writings of Ludwig von Mises, Friedrich Hayek, Milton Friedman, and other free-market prophets.

Sadly, here in the United States, many are still reluctant to end central planning and economic regulation. Despite the spectacular failure of *every* variety of planned economy — and the poverty, misery, and repression caused by those failed experiments in economic coercion — many politicians, intellectuals, and policy makers still are unwilling to embrace true economic freedom for America.

REDUCE GOVERNMENT, INCREASE LIBERTY AND PRODUCTIVITY

The lack of true economic freedom makes Americans poorer. Every reduction in taxes — and every decrease in government control over economic activity — would improve America's productivity and increase employment. This would result in a faster-rising standard of living for everybody. It would also mean a much wider variety of choices and opportunities for all persons, of every income level, to improve their own conditions.

Why do reduced taxes improve economic productivity? The answer illuminates the difference between freedom and coercion.

When people voluntarily make an agreement, and freely negotiate the terms of an economic transaction, the deal they make benefits *them* (from their own point of view, of course). If they didn't think the deal would benefit them, they wouldn't make it. Obviously, some decisions and investments don't turn out as successfully as people hope. Some businesses go bust. However, when private individuals or companies fail, the loss is their own. Others are not obligated to bail them out. Individuals learn from their mistakes, and move on.

Government is different. Government bureaucracies are not subject to a profit-and-loss statement. Nor do governments have the incentive of market competition to make them more efficient. Nor do governments have to keep "customers" happy to remain in business. Even if you don't want a government service, you can be forced to pay for it. When a government program fails, politicians simply require taxpayers to subsidize the loss. And when a government program fails, politicians will frequently claim the program was "underfunded," and demand higher taxes to try again. So, when government makes bad decisions, those decisions cost more, last longer, and affect more people.

Government waste is a universal phenomenon and a necessary consequence of bureaucracy. Just as in socialist economies, officials running U.S. government bureaucracies have little incentive to use resources efficiently. Most government decisions are made for *political* reasons — to satisfy special-interest groups or particular blocs of voters. Decisions are *not* made for economic reasons — to satisfy the greatest number of voluntary customers of a particular good or service.

It gets worse. Government officials typically want their agencies to increase in mission scope, number of employees, and budget. That is how bureaucrats measure "success." The bigger their department, the more important they are. The natural impulse of *any* government program, agency, or department is to grow ever larger. That's why Ronald Reagan once quipped, " A government bureau is the nearest thing to eternal life we'll ever see on this earth."

Given its perverse incentives, not even angels could operate a bureaucracy efficiently. So when politicians tax away the earnings of people in the private sector and transfer their wealth to government bureaucrats who use it in a less-efficient manner, the total economic pie shrinks. Money that could have created jobs and new business is frittered away on wasteful government programs.

Therefore, reducing taxes helps us all. Eliminating regulations creates economic growth that benefits every American. Productivity will increase. Jobs will be created. More people will be able to find work doing the things they enjoy; jobs that give them the best opportunity to improve their conditions in accordance with their values.

Without economic liberty, citizens remain poor and easily controlled by government. Without personal liberty, citizens live in fear of their government. With neither economic nor personal liberty, the result is the poverty and repression that devastated countries like North Korea, Zimbabwe, and Uzbekistan. Only with both — economic liberty *and* personal liberty — can countries prosper, economies thrive, and individuals lead happy, autonomous, fulfilling lives.

In other words, economic liberty and personal liberty are inseparable.

CHAPTER FOURTEEN

POLLUTION AND ENVIRONMENTAL VALUES

Everyone expresses great concern about "pollution" and "the environment." Most have only a hazy grasp of what they are talking about, but the level of concern is quite high. It will help, therefore, to define these terms.

"Pollution" refers to the act of some person (or group) who removes something he does not want from his property, usually something unhealthy, unpleasant, or both, and dumps it on some other property without the consent of the owner of that property.

"Environment" is a confusing term as it is commonly used, because it refers to "everything out there." It will clarify matters to think simply of all the property in the world, whether owned by individuals, companies, or some government. It will become clear that the difference in the way property is treated depends a great deal on whether it is privately owned or is under government ownership.

Environmental issues cover a wide range of concerns, such as: pollution of air or water, maintaining wilderness, protection of endangered species or other wildlife, timber or grazing lands, water rights, and mining. All of these things have value to many people. There is dispute, however, over priorities and how decisions are to be made.

THE CHOICE: PRIVATE PROPERTY OR BUREAUCRACY

The choice is between two different legal frameworks. One is the bureaucratic management model best represented by the federal Environmental Protection Agency (EPA), the U.S. Forest Service, and the Bureau of Land Management. Many Americans assume that without these agencies our water and air would be fouled hopelessly. Or that private developers would bulldoze the national parks and replace them with shopping malls, condominiums, and parking lots.

The alternative legal framework is the traditional Anglo-American system of private property under which private citizens can acquire, establish, protect, and exchange rights in property of all forms. In such a system, government's function is to protect the citizens' property rights, not to regulate their use. Neither of these options is perfect. Utopia is not an option. But the private property-based system, if allowed to work, does a much better job of protecting environmental values.

Many Americans don't understand how our present situation works. First, people typically assume that polluters can only be stopped by regulatory officials working for the EPA or similar agencies. Second, many assume private owners of property have some perverse motivation to destroy its value in the pursuit of short-range profits alone. Third, many people think that only public-spirited bureaucrats can manage forests, grazing lands, or wilderness in a manner that does not destroy their long-term value. Fourth, many assume that there is little cost associated with the system of bureaucratic control. Each of these assumptions is false, as we shall see.

POLLUTION IS A TRESPASS

To help understand pollution issues, consider the following simple example. If a person takes his trash to his property line and dumps it over the fence into his neighbor's yard, that conduct is clearly a "trespass." We would all justifiably expect the law to provide a remedy to the victim.

In fact, our law has, for centuries, provided two effective remedies. The injured party can sue for an injunction to prevent any further polluting conduct. He can also recover monetary damages for any injury already done to his property. Pollution should be analyzed as a matter of common-law trespass; that is, one person or group dumping trash on another's property without consent.

The pollution problems we usually hear about are just more complex factual situations. Air pollution involves some persons or companies putting airborne trash into the atmosphere where it travels to and invades the property of others, including their most fundamental property — their bodies. Water pollution involves some persons or companies dumping trash into water that doesn't belong to them. Toxic waste problems often involve product wastes buried in the ground that migrate across property lines.

A major contributing factor to the problem of water pollution is that the government owns the waterways; private ownership of rivers, lakes, and streams no longer exists in America, for all practical purposes. Government has allowed polluters to foul the water, whereas a private owner of water rights in a lake or river would have much greater incentive to bring effective legal action to stop polluters. There is no good reason why government should be the owner of lakes and rivers. Waterways should be sold into private ownership. In the United Kingdom, for example, fishing rights in rivers are privately owned, and the Anglers Cooperative Association (ACA) sues upstream polluters who damage fish stocks. Over the years, the organization has filed more than 1,500 lawsuits and collected a considerable amount of money in damages. The ACA's actions also had "a profound effect on the attitude of industry, local authorities, and politicians," reported a Cato Institute Policy Analysis. A similar policy in the United States would greatly improve the prospects for action to reduce water pollution.

TOXIC WASTES

Toxic waste is also a problem best analyzed as a trespass. If toxic chemicals are buried and then travel underground to the property of other persons, the victims should have legal redress against those who did the dumping. Unfortunately, having the right to a legal remedy does not always mean the victim will be made whole. Sometimes polluters become "judgment proof" by going bankrupt or just disappearing. (Judgment-proof defendants are found in many situations, not just where toxic wastes or other environmental issues are concerned.)

But if a person's property suffers damage by toxic waste, that does not justify having the government force other people to pay — through taxes — to clean up the mess, even where the wrongdoer is judgment proof. The so called federal "Superfund," purportedly designed to pay for toxic waste cleanup, is really a subsidy for companies that have dumped wastes, for people whose property has been damaged by them, for the companies paid to do the work, and for the bureaucrats who run it. The program actually encourages environmental irresponsibility by sending the message that the government will bail you out of your toxic waste problem. Once again, the taxpayers get stuck with the bill.

BUREAUCRACY IS POOR PROTECTION

Bureaucratic management magnifies and aggravates pollution problems. Bureaucratic decisions are political. So those with the most political clout tend to get their way. Often these are the same people the bureaucracy was set up to control. Who is likely to have more money to lobby the politicians: big business or the environmentalists?

If the courts would recognize the right of private citizens to sue air polluters on the basis of trespass against their bodies and other property, the air would be much cleaner than it is today.

Since the dawn of the glasnost era in the former Soviet Union and Eastern Europe, the world has learned that the environment suffered grievously under socialism — much more so than in the West where the legal systems are more respectful of private property. Lakes, rivers, and the air are so foul in some places in the former Soviet Union and Eastern Europe that people are chronically ill and life expectancy is dropping. This is a lesson for those who urge more centralized government control to "protect" the environment. Central "planning" destroys an economy. It also destroys the environment, and for the same reasons.

SOVEREIGN IMMUNITY

Another aggravating factor is the principle of "sovereign immunity." This legal principle prevents lawsuits by citizens against the government, except where the government consents to be sued.

This is particularly troubling because the federal government is "the worst polluter in the land," according to a 1999 report by the *Boston Globe*. The newspaper found that EPA laboratories in Massachusetts leaked mercury into ground water; the Park Service dumped "tens of thousands of gallons of raw sewage" in Yellowstone National Park; and the Department of Energy polluted 475 billion gallons of ground water and created 113 radioactive sites. In all, the government contaminated at least 61,155 locations around the United States, the *Globe* reported.

The cost to clean up the environmental devastation done by federal agencies and the military could exceed $300 billion — five times the cost of all the environmental harm done by chemical and oil companies. But because of sovereign immunity, private citizens have no legal redress. Not a single government official will face criminal charges or jail time for the environmental damage they authorized. Remarkably, the fact that the federal government is the nation's greatest environmental villain has not stopped activists from reflexively turning to politicians to "protect the environment."

Respect for private property rights in the legal system and repeal of the doctrine of sovereign immunity would give local citizens the tools to accelerate cleaning up the environment. Privatization of government-owned power plants and sewage treatment facilities would not only improve their efficiency and lower costs to consumers, it would eliminate the obstacle to environmental protection created by the doctrine of sovereign immunity.

BUREAUCRACY GENERATES LITIGATION

Some people believe that replacing the bureaucratic system with a private property-based system would generate much litigation over environmental issues. The mistake here is to forget that our current bureaucratic system requires hosts of lawyers, both within government regulatory agencies and on the staffs of the regulated companies.

Environmental lawsuits are a great drain on productivity. Today, any proposed construction project can be delayed or stopped entirely by litigation in the name of the environment. Examples abound. In northern California, union activists filed environmental lawsuits against WalMart to stop the construction of new stores in 30 cities. (Not coincidentally, the activists opposed WalMart's policy of hiring non-union workers.) In Washington state, environmental lawsuits delayed the construction of a new runway at Sea-Tac Airport by more than a decade, and helped add $1 billion to the price tag. In Calabasas, California, environmental lawsuits delayed by at least 11 years a plan to build 3,050 new homes. As the *Contra Costa Times* noted, California environmental law is "open to those who would use — or abuse — the legal system to prevent new housing from being built, or delay it." Consumers end up paying more for houses (and everything else) because business must cover the cost of actual or potential environmental litigation in everything produced and sold.

By contrast, where property rights are clearly delineated, there is less litigation because potential litigants can more easily determine what is and is not permissible.

PRIVATE RESOURCE MANAGEMENT WORKS BETTER THAN BUREAUCRACY

The U.S. government owns approximately one-third of the land in this country, most of it in the West and the Southwest. Some of it is Indian reservations, some national parks, some forests and grazing lands, some wilderness. The government also owns the outer continental shelf, an underwater shelf along our coastlines which contains oil and other mineral wealth. Many environmentalists express concern that if private owners were to get their hands on any of it, terrible things would happen. Those concerns may be understandable, but they are largely in error. More environmental damage occurs under government management than from private ownership.

As with any bureaucracy, government land managers have no effective way to know the relative values of different uses, because no market-pricing system can develop. People with different ideas about how to use publicly owned resources cannot bid against each other to show which uses people value more than others. Without the guide of market pricing, bureaucrats and legislators base their decisions on political considerations. So, the people with political clout typically prevail and taxpayers foot the bill. As the Property and Environment Research Center has noted: "Although the federal government manages a wealth of natural resources, it consistently loses money on timber, grazing, and recreation."

Horror stories about overlogging and overgrazing usually turn out, upon examination, to be stories of bureaucratic mismanagement of government-owned forest and grazing land. This does not mean that private companies do not sometimes purchase the right to log or graze on government land and overuse it. But that conduct is a rational response to government contracts that create those very incentives. The government land managers simply do a poor job of protecting the public trust. The U.S. Forest Service often builds logging roads, at taxpayer expense, into national forests. This is merely a subsidy for logging companies. The Forest Service has traditionally not required logging companies to pay full value for trees cut on public land.

Bureaucratic managers have no incentive to take a long-range view and cannot personally benefit from increasing the value of what they control. They personally pay no penalty for bad (economically inefficient) decisions. By contrast, private owners are disciplined by the market. If they invest in improving their property, such as with pollution-control equipment, the market value increases. Or, if they allow it to be polluted, overgrazed, or strip mined, it will lose value. Because of the incentives inherent in the bureaucratic system, government officials are more interested in accumulating political power and increasing their budgets than in enhancing the economic value of the property they control.

Private owners of timber lands have a strong incentive to replenish the forest so as to maintain the land at its highest value in the long run. It is no accident that timber companies like Weyerhauser and Georgia Pacific do a more efficient long-term job of using their forest lands than federal and state governments do with theirs. Such efficient use includes not only logging, but the maintenance of game preserves, camping facilities, and hiking trails. International Paper leases parts of its timber holdings for hunting, fishing, and recreation, and makes a profit doing so. Since World War II, the amount of forest and timberland in the United States has been increasing. This increase is largely because of market demand for lumber and paper. Private timber companies own land to grow trees. They harvest those trees to sell for construction lumber and paper production. They are constantly planting new trees to guarantee a future supply of timber. Instead of destroying trees, the free market and private ownership create incentives to *increase* productive forests. Bureaucratic managers of publicly owned forests do not have the same incentives.

MARKET ENVIRONMENTALISTS AND ENVIRONMENTALIST PROPERTY OWNERS

Worldwide, entrepreneurs are finding ways to use market mechanisms to protect environmental values and make profits. In South Africa, the Conservation Corp., to attract environmentally oriented tourists, is working with landowners to create large habitats for African wildlife, replacing cattle and crops. The Oregon Water Trust raises private donations to purchase water rights from farmers to improve habitat for spawning salmon and steelhead. Similarly, the Atlantic Salmon Federation pays Faroe Islands fisherman not to net salmon at sea in the North Atlantic. Their efforts have doubled the number of salmon in rivers in Iceland and in parts of Europe.

Massive government dams on the Columbia River in the Pacific Northwest reduced salmon populations. The Environmental Defense Fund brokered a deal that resulted in farmers taking less water in exchange for payment from the Bonneville Power Administration (BPA). The heightened water levels permitted the BPA to generate more power — and allowed salmon to more easily swim upriver to spawn. Both sides win and the salmon benefit most.

Many environmental and conservation organizations also own forest and wilderness land. The National Audubon Society operates

100 wildlife sanctuaries and nature centers. It owns Rainey Wildlife Sanctuary in Louisiana, a 26,000-acre sanctuary for animals, reptiles, and birds. Royalties from oil and natural gas wells in the sanctuary pay for its operation.

The Nature Conservancy has more than 1,340 sanctuaries and has helped protect more than 12 million acres in the United States. It identifies areas of unique value and raises funds to purchase them. One such purchase was Santa Cruz Island, off California. It would probably surprise most people to learn that the major contributors to the Nature Conservancy projects are the very same "big corporations" so many accuse of being environmental destroyers.

Ducks Unlimited protects more than a million acres of wildlands each year through easements that preserve waterfowl habitats. Operation Stronghold is a national association of private landowners who manage their land in ways that protect or enhance wildlife habitat.

Increasingly, environmental groups have come to the view that private ownership is the best way for them to accomplish their objectives. Keeping in mind that the government operates the lands it owns at a loss, it would be a benefit to the taxpayer if the law allowed organizations like the Nature Conservancy, Wilderness Society, and Sierra Club to purchase government land that fits their special expertise and concern.

The traditional private property system provides the simplest, fairest way for people holding different values to reach agreement on property use. For example, environmentalists who want to save old-growth trees on private property should offer to purchase the property and bear the cost of preserving what they think is important. That's a better solution than using the government to deprive the owners of the economic value of their timber.

PERVERSE RESULTS OF BUREAUCRACY

Reliance on government to "protect the environment" leads to perverse results and perpetual conflict. Virtually anyone can halt logging, mining, oil recovery, construction of homes, or highways by bringing lawsuits that go on for years. Some environmentalists give a colony of spotted owls a higher priority than the jobs of thousands of loggers and construction workers, or the homes that might be built for thousands of families with lumber from trees that can't be cut.

Some extreme environmentalists go even further. In *The End of Nature,* Bill McKibben writes that humans are "a plague upon ourselves and upon the earth... Some of us can only hope for the right virus to come along." Such extremists call for laws to prevent humans from making any change in the "natural" environment. (The natural environment they seek to protect is one that humans, including Native Americans, have been altering for thousands of years. How far back do they want to go?)

The most radical environmentalists believe everything humans have ever done to improve living conditions for our species on this earth has been a disaster and should be undone so that all other species, plant, animal, insect and virus, can go on without the blight of *homo sapiens* to cause them distress. In his book *Green Rage,* Christopher Manes even calls for "the reduction of the human population to an ecologically sustainable level." He doesn't say how many millions — or billions — of people would have to die to achieve that state of imagined environmental utopianism.

While such extremism is rare, it does have an impact on how people view the environment, economic progress, and property rights. Today, the person who has the least to say about what can be done on a parcel of private property is often the person who owns it. And where government property is concerned, the politicized bureaucratic system ensures a never-ending series of conflicts, lawsuits, and vigilante violence.

CONCLUSION

For anyone concerned about pollution, wilderness, endangered species, or other environmental issues, privatization and the protection of property rights holds much more promise than inept management by government bureaucracy. Neither bureaucratic management nor the free-market system, grounded in legally protected and exchangeable private property rights, provides a perfect solution. But the private property framework clearly provides the best available set of tools to implement the most rational and productive use of our environment, in the interest of all the people, now and in the future.

CHAPTER FIFTEEN

GUNS, CRIME AND PERSONAL RESPONSIBILITY

Americans want to be able to walk city streets without fear and to feel secure in their homes. All too frequently, the fear of crime prevents that.

Criminals often use guns in their criminal activity, even in states and cities where gun ownership is banned or strictly limited. In most states it is a crime for persons previously convicted of serious crime to possess any firearm. Yet career criminals obtain guns and use them in later crimes. Gun-control laws are obviously ineffective at keeping guns out of the hands of criminals.

Some people erroneously conclude that guns themselves cause trouble. They compound the error by claiming that depriving all private citizens of guns would end all crime, homicides, and injury caused by criminals or negligent gun owners. Some others simply don't like guns, can't understand how anyone could, and will seize on any opportunity to stop gun ownership for everyone — except for government employees.

THE SECOND AMENDMENT

Fortunately, the U.S. Constitution has something to say on this subject. The Second Amendment states:

> *A well-regulated militia being necessary to the security of a free State, the right of the people to keep and bear arms shall not be infringed.*

Peaceful, law-abiding people have reason to defend that right to "keep and bear arms." To the patriots of the American Revolution, one reason was paramount. They demanded a Bill of

Rights, including the Second Amendment, before ratifying the Constitution. They wanted to control the new national government, and limit the inevitable tendency of governments to grow and become oppressors of their own citizens, as had the British government. They knew that without firearms, they could not hope to resist potential future government tyranny. The right to revolt against tyranny would mean little without guns in the hands of freedom-loving people.

The concern of the American revolutionaries was justified, and is validated by history. Around the world, dictators and authoritarian governments invariably seek to disarm the people to consolidate their power and to deprive the resistance of any hope of success.

The right to keep and bear arms protected by the Second Amendment is a personal, *individual* right. Founding Father James Madison wrote that all ten amendments in the Bill of Rights were "calculated to secure the personal rights of the people." However, in recent decades, federal courts have perverted the Second Amendment, holding that the right protected is the right of state governments to have a militia, such as the National Guard. An avalanche of legal and historical scholarship demonstrates unequivocally that these court decisions are wrong. In 2004, even the U.S. Department of Justice concluded that "the Second Amendment secures a personal right of individuals, not a collective right that may only be invoked by a State or a quasi-collective right restricted to those persons who serve in organized militia units."

When the Second Amendment was adopted, there was no doubt that the right was personal and that the "militia" was every adult male who might be called upon to defend against invasion or resist tyranny. In the context of the time, the people refused to ratify the Constitution without a Bill of Rights, including the Second Amendment. The reason was that the people were concerned with the threat to their liberties from *government*.

The Second Amendment was adopted by the people to defend against the risk that their newly created government might become as oppressive as the British government had been. In many state and federal court cases in the early history of the country, it was clearly accepted that the right to keep and bear arms was an individual right.

BASIC HUMAN RIGHTS

There is an even more fundamental reason than the Constitution to support gun ownership: individual human rights. Mere ownership of a gun violates no other person's rights. If you own a .357 Magnum pistol, a hunting rifle, a shotgun, or a machine gun, it does me no harm. You may own hundreds of guns and the ammunition for them. Doing so violates the rights of no other person. There is no justification for making you a criminal because of that ownership. I must respect your right as a human being, equal to me, to own, possess, or use any property you have acquired peacefully and honestly. Period. Including guns.

Your reasons for owning a firearm are irrelevant. It doesn't matter if you have it for a personal protection, hunting, investment, competition shooting, collecting, or because you inherited it from a beloved grandparent. So long as you harm no other person, no one has the right to complain. It's your business alone.

Gun-control advocates care nothing for your constitutional rights or your right to control your own life and property. Indeed, they use the term "gun control" to focus attention on the inanimate object and the harm it can do, to disguise the fact that what they really want is to control other human beings, violating their rights in the process.

THE PROHIBITION LESSON

Gun-control advocates resemble the alcohol prohibitionists of the early 20th century. By making liquor illegal, they spawned organized crime, caused bloody, violent turf wars, and corrupted the criminal justice system. It is the same today with the War on Drugs. Prohibition didn't stop liquor use; the drug laws can't stop drug use. Criminalizing gun ownership will also inevitably fail. People will always seek effective ways to defend themselves, so there will always be a demand for guns. Laws making gun ownership a crime will only drive that demand underground. It will never eliminate it. Nor will it prevent the demand from being supplied by sellers willing to operate in the black market.

The innocent victim of misguided gun-control efforts will be the honest citizen whose civil rights are trampled as frustrated legislators and police tighten the screws, as they are doing with the Drug War. Banning guns will only make guns more expensive and give organized crime greater opportunities to make profits in the black market for weapons. Street violence will increase in new turf wars. Criminals will not give up their guns. But many law-abiding citizens will, leaving them defenseless against armed criminals. Consider Washington, DC. After that city banned handguns in 1976, the homicide rate skyrocketed by 200% over the next 16 years.

PERSONAL SECURITY

Americans have the right to decide how best to protect themselves, their families, and their property. Millions of Americans have guns in their homes and sleep more comfortably because of it. Studies show that where it is against the law for citizens to own guns, criminals commit more residential burglaries. No one has anything to fear from the person who keeps a gun in his or her home for protection — except burglars.

Police don't have the resources to provide on-the-spot security in your home, your business, or the street. They show up after the crime to take reports and do detective work, usually unsuccessfully. The poorer the neighborhood, the riskier it is for residents who seek to live peacefully and mind their own business. Gun ownership may not only be their first, but their sole, line of defense. Guns are also the safest way to protect yourself against crime. Gary Kleck, writing in *Point Blank* (1991), cites a National Crime Victimization Survey that revealed that "robbery and assault victims who used a gun to resist were less likely to be attacked or to suffer an injury than those who used any other methods of self-protection or those who did not resist at all."

Gun controllers frequently target inexpensive handguns, calling them "Saturday night specials." That label is supposed to make them more ominous. Banning such guns, they contend, will reduce crime. All it will actually do is make it more difficult for the law-abiding poor in crime-ridden cities to protect themselves. That's why gun-rights advocate Alan Korwin suggests that when gun-controllers talk about banning "Saturday night specials," you should point out that such a racist law would deny affordable guns to poor people. As Korwin notes: "A woman who eats inexpensive food and drives an inexpensive car doesn't lose her right to protect her family because she can only afford an inexpensive gun."

ARMED CITIZENS DETER CRIME

Only an armed citizenry can be present in sufficient numbers to prevent or deter violent crime, or to reduce its spread. Interviews with convicted felons indicate that fear of armed citizens deters crime. A study by the U.S. Department of Justice found that as many as 40% of felons decided not to commit a particular crime for fear their potential victim was armed. This makes sense. If a holdup man knows that the clerk and many of the customers in a convenience store might be armed, he will probably decide the risk to his own life is too great to attempt a robbery.

Statistically, a criminal is more likely to be driven off from a particular crime by an armed citizen than to be convicted and imprisoned for it. A study by criminologist Gary Kleck (published in the *Journal of Criminal Law and Criminology*, Fall 1995) found that guns were used for protection as many as 2.5 million times a year. Thus, widespread gun ownership makes neighborhoods safer.

In recent years, more and more states have passed laws allowing concealed carrying of firearms. As of 2005, 38 states have such "shall-issue" laws, so called because officials must issue the permit for concealed carry if the citizen is not a felon or otherwise disqualified. This has not led to a "Wild West" atmosphere. Instead, it has led to a decrease in violent crime in those states. A 1996 study (by Dr. John Lott and David Mustard of the University of Chicago) of crime statistics in every U.S. county from 1972 to 1992, shows that, where concealed carry is legal, murders were down

8.5%, rapes 5%, and aggravated assault 7%. This should be no surprise. Criminals are likely to avoid situations where potential victims can carry guns. It is apparent that all of us, including those who do not carry weapons, benefit because the existence of the right-to-carry law deters criminals. If every state adopted shall-issue laws, the same 1996 study estimates that 1,570 murders per year would be avoided, along with 4,200 rapes and 60,000 severe assaults.

Significantly, after a concealed-carry law went into effect in Florida in 1987, violent crime went down, while attacks on foreign tourists increased because criminals knew the tourists cannot be legally armed. But the average person was much safer. In the ten years after Florida passed its concealed-carry law, the state homicide rate fell by 39%. After Texas passed a similar law in 1995, its murder rate dropped by 34% in five years. By contrast, some of the states and cities that have the strictest gun control laws have high levels of violent crime.

Further, only a handful of the hundreds of thousands of citizens issued permits used their guns unlawfully. In Florida, for example, only 19 people in eight years had their gun permits revoked because they committed a crime. Nor should the increased risk of accidental death cause undue alarm. While as many as 175 children under the age of ten tragically die from gun accidents each year, guns have one of the lowest rates of accidental deaths for any potentially dangerous consumer product. For example, economist Steven D. Levitt notes that about 550 children under ten drown in swimming pools each year. Given the relative number of guns and the number of swimming pools in the country, a child is "100 times more likely to die in a swimming pool accident" than from a gun accident, he writes.

On infrequent occasions, a psychotic individual goes on a murderous rampage, usually with a gun he holds illegally. The gun controllers typically respond by calling for more laws restricting everyone else's right to own guns. Such an event led to the 1994 federal ban on 19 types of "assault rifles" and similar bans in some states. "Assault rifle" is an intentionally misleading label. The banned guns were standard semi-automatic rifles that require one trigger pull for each shot — not machine guns. They merely are designed to look like military weapons. Gun-control advocates also lied in asserting that these were the weapons of choice for drug dealers and other street criminals. In fact, they were used in less than one percent of violent crime. (The federal "assault weapons" ban expired in 2004.)

Tens of millions of legal gun owners live in America. Of that group, an overwhelming percentage never harm another human being by wrongful or negligent use of their guns. Making gun ownership a crime will make criminals out of millions of law-abiding Americans who are no threat to anyone except criminals. To stigmatize such innocent people with a criminal label would be a moral outrage.

THE DRUG WAR ATTACK ON GUN OWNERSHIP

The "War on Drugs" is undermining the constitutional right to keep and bear arms. In the past, law enforcement personnel typically supported private gun ownership. The drug laws have, inevitably, increased violence among drug dealers fighting over turf. These criminals care nothing about drug laws or gun laws. They have no qualms about using any kind of weaponry, legal or illegal, including military hardware. Now, increasing numbers of unthinking police officials are joining the gun control chorus, even to the point of saying only police should have guns.

The gun controllers would like to make guns, gun owners, and gun manufacturers into scapegoats for any evil that exists in our society, just as drugs, drug users, and drug dealers have been made into scapegoats. The media typically play along by detailing the weapons seized in police raids and referring to any collection of more than one gun as an "arsenal." Monstrous violations of civil rights by the federal government are rationalized on the basis of the size of gun collections, such as the disaster at Waco that incinerated scores of Branch Davidians, including women and children. The gun controllers' strategy is to merge Drug War violence and private gun ownership into one dangerous and evil circumstance in the mind of the public so the gullible will be persuaded that we should give up our rights to both.

This isn't the first time such a strategy has been used. After alcohol Prohibition spawned criminals like Al Capone and led to a surge in gang-related gun violence, politicians responded by passing the National Firearms Act of 1934 and the Federal Firearms Act of 1938. (When Prohibition was repealed, those gun laws stayed on the books.)

Advocates of the right to keep and bear arms have traditionally supported the police and strict enforcement of the drug laws. They must recognize that the gun controllers are using the War on Drugs as a tool to advance their plans to disarm gun owners. As *The Freeman* editor Sheldon Richman notes, "To the extent that conservatives have encouraged the government in the War on Drugs, they have unwittingly helped advance the war on guns. Their enthusiasm for anti-drug laws contributes to the conditions that make some people eager to accept anti-gun laws." Liberty is indivisible. Anyone who claims the right to keep and bear arms must also respect and support the right of other peaceful people to own and use marijuana, cocaine, and heroin.

THE SOLUTION: PERSONAL RESPONSIBILITY

What is the answer? Personal responsibility. Let us not forget that guns are inanimate objects. Only the people who use them can do harm with them. No gun can run amok on its own.

Peaceful, responsible gun ownership and use should not be the subject of any criminal law or legal restriction. Law-abiding, responsible citizens should not need to ask anyone's permission to engage in a peaceful activity. Gun ownership by itself harms no other person and cannot morally justify criminal penalties.

Rather than banning guns, politicians and the police should encourage responsible gun ownership, as well as education and gun-safety training. We should applaud organizations, such as the National Rifle Association, that offer programs teaching safe firearm ownership, care, and use.

Conversely, the use of a gun to commit a crime or to threaten other persons should subject the user to severe criminal penalties.

In fact, our laws already carry such penalties. It is only the failure of the federal and state governments to enforce many of the 20,000 gun laws already on the books that allows the gun controllers to argue that more laws are needed.

Further, those who allow harm to come to others through their negligent use or control of firearms in their possession should also bear the consequences under applicable rules of civil liability.

For their own protection, citizens in every state should demand lawmakers pass a "shall-issue" law. Officials must be required to issue permits for concealed carry to every law-abiding citizen who demonstrates competency with firearms. Further, we must demand that the Congress repeal existing federal laws which infringe on the right to keep and bear arms, such as the Brady Bill.

A responsible, well-armed, and trained citizenry is the best protection against domestic crime, potential tyrannical government, and the threat of foreign invasion. America's Founders knew that well. It is still true today.

CHAPTER 16

THE THERAPEUTIC STATE

The "health-care crisis" dominates public debate. Politicians want to get the government more involved in how doctors, hospitals, pharmaceutical companies, and insurance companies operate. Health-care experts hold different views, some calling for more, some less, government funding or regulation of the medical marketplace.

Reporting usually comes in crisis mode. Millions have no health insurance! Medical costs are rising rapidly! Doctors are quitting because medical malpractice insurance is too high! HMOs are out of control! Medicare is the fastest-rising expense in the federal budget! Drug companies make huge profits! Hospital emergency rooms are overcrowded!

No one disputes the value of good health or denies that access to medical treatment is an important factor in achieving it. How did so many things in our system of medicine get so out of whack? What can we do about it?

AVOIDING CONFUSION

Let's first dispose of some persistent errors and face reality. There is no free lunch, and no free medical care. Doctors, nurses, hospitals, and Medicare bureaucrats don't work for free. If those who receive medical care don't pay for it themselves, then someone else must pay for it with tax dollars, higher insurance premiums, or higher hospital and physician's fees.

No one has a "right" to medical care. I have no right to claim that others must pay for my medical care. The self-ownership principle will not allow me to make such a claim. I cannot morally force others to pay for *any* of my wants or needs. The mistaken view that medical care is a "right" is a major source of the chaos in today's medical environment.

Government control (socialism) cannot improve our medical system any more than it improved the economies of the Soviet Union and Eastern Europe. Health care involves millions of providers and consumers engaging in billions of transactions daily. It could function quite well in the free market, but has not been allowed to do so.

American medicine is already heavily regulated by hundreds of federal, state, and local agencies. Governments operate major hospitals, including those run by the Veterans Administration and county governments. These institutions — and the patients in them — suffer from the inevitable problems socialism creates. Legislators and bureaucrats cannot know how to direct scarce medical resources to where they will do the most good for the people who count — the patients. Instead, politicians make *political* decisions that will best help them get re-elected.

There are no perfect solutions. Utopia is not an option. Human beings invariably suffer ailments and injuries. Medical care cannot change that. It can only help in limited ways. Our society is aging. Older people require more medical attention, hospitalization, and medicine.

Finally, doctors, hospitals, drug companies, and other medical professionals are not evil because they require payment for their services. It is a mistake to turn against the dedicated practitioners who provide care and treatment, or to call for bureaucrats to control them. Increasing government interference in medicine will only drive good people out of medicine and discourage talented young people from entering it.

THE THERAPEUTIC STATE

Government policy and an accepting American public have created a "therapeutic state." State power is joined with the medical establishment and deprives ordinary citizens of the right to control their own treatment. Only state-approved persons, "doctors," may give medical advice or treatment. Only state-approved substances, "medicine," may be used and only state-licensed doctors may prescribe them.

Similarly, the terms "illness" and "treatment" have expanded to cover more aspects of life, so that virtually any human activity is subject to control by medical intervention, enforced by law. Consider children. Many school-age children who years ago were called "high energy" are now diagnosed as suffering from a disease — attention deficit disorder (ADD). Many government schools require over-active children to take Ritalin to stay in school. In some cases, school bureaucrats have charged parents with child abuse for taking their child off that psychotropic medication. Loss of liberty and of personal autonomy necessarily follows the mandated medicalization of society.

The Founders of this country understood the value of keeping church and state separate. They understood that when religion is joined with state power, people suffer a loss of freedom and denial of the right to free inquiry. It is equally important to separate medicine and state for the same reasons.

The first step toward improving health care is to reject the view that Big Brother bureaucrats know best. We must demand the right to be responsible for our own treatment and medication decisions.

SOME MEDICAL HISTORY

Nineteenth-century medicine was primitive. Anesthesia was in its infancy and antibiotics unknown. Ignorance of the importance of sterile conditions meant infection killed many. Surgery was rare and dangerous. Epidemics were common; immunizing vaccines unknown. X-ray technology had yet to arrive. Home treatment was frequently safer than hospital treatment. People medicated themselves legally with over-the-counter drugs.

In these circumstances, physicians could do little but provide rudimentary care and advice. No license was required to practice medicine. Patients dealt directly with physicians, participating in treatment decisions and negotiating over fees.

THE AMA MONOPOLY

Wide-open access to the medical profession led established physicians to create the American Medical Association. The AMA made clear that its primary purpose was to limit the number of new doctors so that working doctors could make more money.

Early in the 20th century, the AMA moved to control medical schools by granting or withholding its approval of their programs and operations. Many existing medical schools (including many that trained black doctors) closed after being denied approval. Fewer spots were available in medical schools for aspiring doctors.

The AMA's plan could not succeed without government help. State legislatures cooperated by passing laws requiring graduation from an AMA-approved medical school in order to practice medicine. Medical licensing was born.

While lobbying for their legal monopoly, AMA spokespeople cloaked their true motivations in public-interest language. "We want to protect the ignorant public from quacks and charlatans who lack proper medical training and ethics," they claimed. The government medical bureaucracy makes the same argument. It is a lie. Medical licensing has little to do with quality medical care. It has everything to do with limiting and controlling health care and medical advice.

THE FOOD AND DRUG ADMINISTRATION

Congress created the modern version of the Food and Drug Administration (FDA) in 1906 after sensational disclosures of sanitation problems in the meat-packing industry. With regard to pharmaceutical drugs, until 1962 the FDA required only that they be safe. Since 1962, they must be proven safe and effective for a specified purpose.

The 1962 FDA regulation caused untold illness and early death, along with inflated costs. The Cato Institute estimates that it takes as long as 15 years to get a new drug approved by the FDA. And it costs $880 million to bring a new drug to market, according to figures cited in 2002 by the Institute for Policy Innovation. The result is that many life-saving medicines, available in other countries, are denied to Americans. The most famous example may be beta blocker drugs. As many as 119,000 Americans died because of the FDA's seven-year delay in approving that heart-attack medicine, according to Dr. Louis Lasagna, director of Tufts University's Center for the Study of Drug Development.

The AIDS crisis further illuminated the problem. In the 1980s, AIDS activists openly imported unapproved AIDS treatment drugs to help victims. They also demonstrated against federal regulations that prohibited treatment options for dying victims. In response, the FDA was forced to streamline its procedures to speed the discovery of AIDS treatments. There is no reason to deny victims of AIDS — or any other disease or condition — the right to control their treatment.

WHAT IS THE PUBLIC INTEREST?

We all want medical practitioners to be well-trained and competent. We want medicine to be pure and effective. What we need is information about medical professionals and the medicines we purchase so we can make informed decisions. That is the public interest.

A government license does not ensure competence. If it did, there would be no medical malpractice lawsuits. Most state licensing is only for the general practitioner. Most medical specialists — such as surgeons, gynecologists, and anesthesiologists — are certified by boards made up of other physicians, not government bureaucrats. When we need treatment, we typically search out specialists by relying on the advice of family, friends, or other physicians we trust. State licenses do little except create a false sense of security.

We don't need the FDA for medical information. Many private businesses already provide information to consumers. Underwriters Laboratories tests and certifies electrical appliances. The American Society for Testing Materials sets standards for thousands of industrial materials. *Consumer Reports* tests hundreds of consumer products. If government left the medical field, existing information businesses would expand to meet the demand for medical information. All you and I would need to do is be responsible patients and make intelligent use of the available information.

MEDICAL INSURANCE:
SEPARATING PATIENT AND DOCTOR

"Medical insurance" is a misnomer. Compare it to automobile insurance. The owner of a car pays for all ordinary maintenance – and insurance only comes into play when a specified risk, such as collision damage or theft, occurs. Most medical insurance is better described as a pre-payment pool for all medical expenses. Typically, the patient pays little or nothing out-of-pocket for medicine, doctor's appointments, or hospitalization. The insurer pays most of the bill.

This system drives up demand and costs. If you pay almost nothing out-of-pocket for medical attention, you will tend to purchase more than if you were paying most or all of the price. The system encourages excessive use by patients, and removes any incentive for doctors and hospitals to trim costs. Again, consider auto insurance. If insurance companies paid the entire cost of routine maintenance, what incentive would you have to shop around for the best deal in oil changes, replacement wiper blades, or new tires?

The insurance system also tends to eliminate price negotiations between doctor and patient. Indeed, many doctors and patients don't know or care what medical services cost. They rely on the insurance company (or Medicare) to pay the bill. Interestingly, when medical procedures are not covered by insurance, such as cosmetic surgery, studies show that patients and doctors *do* negotiate a price for the procedure before proceeding.

TAX EFFECTS ON MEDICAL INSURANCE

Millions of Americans have no medical insurance – primarily because of the federal tax system. Employer-provided medical insurance is tax-deductible to the employer, but is not taxed as employee income. Insurance purchased independently by individuals or the self-employed is *not* tax deductible. If employees change jobs, or are laid off, they frequently lose their coverage. Others make a rational choice not to buy medical insurance because it is too expensive, particularly if the expense is not tax-deductible.

As long as the federal income tax exists, any purchase of medical insurance should be tax-deductible. This would give unemployed or self-employed persons the same tax benefit as those whose employers purchase their insurance. (Unemployed people should be able to claim their tax deduction on future income, once they are employed again.) In addition, all out-of-pocket payments for medical expenses should be tax-deductible.

Another related reform would be to allow an employee's insurance to be transferable from job to job or to unemployed status. The covered employee would not then feel tied to one employer just to retain medical coverage.

BIG-GOVERNMENT MEDICINE

The 1960s saw an explosion of government programs and regulation. That era also saw increasing health-care costs. In 1960, Congress passed legislation to fund medical welfare programs run by the states. In 1965, Congress declared that everyone had a "right" to basic medical care and created Medicare and Medicaid. Medicare pays for direct medical care for the elderly. Medicaid is a combined federal and state program which pays for medical welfare for the poor, regardless of age.

Government has become the single largest purchaser of health care. According to the Cato Institute, government now directly pays 44% of the nation's total health-care costs. The inevitable result has been skyrocketing costs to taxpayers and patients.

Medicare and Medicaid are the fastest-growing parts of the federal budget. By 2030, there will be an estimated 76 million people on Medicare, double today's numbers. Because of our aging population, Medicare and Medicaid face unfunded liabilities of over $30 trillion, and will require increasing amounts of tax dollars to stave off bankruptcy. Politicians will have only two choices: raise taxes by as much as 100% or slash future benefits. This is the inevitable consequence of socialism in medicine.

Greater government involvement means more regulation and cost. Insurance companies are required to include coverage for every kind of physical and mental complaint. According to the *Cato Handbook on Policy*, "states have enacted 1,823 separate requirements that insurance cover particular items." Such requirements drive up the cost of insurance for everyone. Insurance companies can also be prohibited by law from raising the price of insurance to certain groups of high-risk people. So people with good health habits subsidize the medical costs of risky behavior like smoking, sedentary lifestyles, and obesity. Hospitals are required by law to treat anyone who comes in the door of emergency rooms, even if they cannot pay. So emergency rooms have become primary treatment centers for the poor.

THE MEDICAL MALPRACTICE CRISIS

The cost of medical care has gone up because of huge damage awards to plaintiffs in medical malpractice cases, which increases the cost of malpractice insurance. (Of course, malpractice does sometimes occur, and injured parties should be compensated by those who negligently caused their injuries.)

In some specialties, e.g., obstetrics, many doctors have stopped practicing because they cannot afford the insurance. This shortage of qualified physicians in certain specialties leaves some patients unserved and raises the price to others.

In some states, legislators have capped malpractice awards. But this price-fixing does not solve the root problem, which is, again, the separation of patient and provider. People have come to believe that they are entitled to "perfect" medical results. By excluding patients from significant participation in medical decisions, physicians have contributed to the view that they are all-knowing. So if things don't turn out right, patients frequently assume the doctor erred and sue for damages.

This helps explain increasing medical costs caused by advancing technology. The legal standard for professional malpractice is whether the professional performed according to the "ordinary and customary" practices of the field. But with doctors, juries tend to hold them to a higher standard. They want doctors to use *every* diagnostic test available. Consequently, physicians subject us to an unreasonable number of expensive tests to avoid potential malpractice liability.

MORE SOCIALISM WILL MAKE THINGS WORSE

Today's medical situation may be the most complicated of our domestic issues. Unfortunately, few politicians are willing to ask whether government involvement is the *source* of the problems.

Some current political proposals include: a national tax-paid medical insurance program to cover uninsured people; laws requiring all employers to provide medical insurance for employees; government fixing of prices for doctor's fees and other medical services; and limiting the number of medical procedures covered by Medicare and Medicaid. Some even propose that we adopt a system of completely socialized medicine, like the one in Canada.

It's time our politicians admitted that socialism fails wherever it is tried. All socialist medical systems claim to give "free" care. But we know that nothing is free. Socialist medicine tends to be substandard, as we can see from Veterans Administration hospitals, county hospitals, and government medical care on Indian reservations. Despite the government-caused problem in our system, America still has the highest-quality health care in the world. Americans would be very unhappy if access to that care was limited, or if the quality of care declined further.

Socialized medicine rations access to hospitals and treatment. Patients wait months for hospital admissions for most non-emergency procedures. In Canada, the average wait for specialized treatment is 17.7 weeks, according to economist Walter E. Williams. In the U.S., patients seeking treatment are admitted with little or no delay. Many Canadians come to the U.S. for treatment, happily paying the extra price for faster treatment.

Other proposed government interventions will only aggravate matters. Price-fixing by government — that is, putting an upper limit on what suppliers can charge — always results in a reduction of supply and quality. For example, pharmaceutical companies spend billions of dollars every year to research new medicines. If government limits the prices they can charge, investors will not put money into those companies, and they will have less money for research. The result will be fewer improvements in medicine, more illness, and an increased number of unnecessary deaths.

Another example. If government requires all employers to offer a medical plan for their employees, unemployment will increase. Many small companies will be unable to afford the extra cost and will hire fewer employees or will close their doors. People considering opening a new business may not do so after factoring in the cost of mandated employee medical insurance.

MEDICAL IRAS AND SAVINGS ACCOUNTS

Two sensible tax law proposals would help shift medical decisions back towards the consumer. The Medical Individual Retirement Account (MIRA) would expand on existing IRAs. Currently, workers can put $2,000 per year tax-free into an IRA. The interest it earns is tax-free. Upon retirement, people can draw money from the IRA and pay taxes then (usually at lower rates because the retiree's income is lower). The MIRA concept lets workers save money tax-free during their working years so it will be available for medical purposes after retirement.

The medical savings ("Medisave") account addresses workers' current medical expenses. Under this proposal, workers could put tax-free earnings into a savings account and withdraw funds for catastrophic medical needs. Workers could not draw on the Medisave account for ordinary medical expenses. Under both the MIRA and the Medisave proposal, the individual benefits by an immediate tax reduction, and by the fact that the money remains his. Upon death, it passes to his heirs, unlike Medicare taxes.

SOME LIBERTARIAN APPROACHES

There is no Utopian solution to the medical-care mess. But we can make matters better by reducing government involvement and by adopting policies to return control to patients.

1. Provide tax breaks for medical insurance and expenses paid by individuals.

As a first step, and an interim proposal for so long as the federal income tax exists, the tax code could give a tax credit for a portion of the medical expenses paid by the individual, including the cost of insurance. (A tax credit is a dollar-for-dollar reduction in your tax bill.) The tax credit would allow more people to afford medical insurance, particularly those who do not get it as an employment benefit. The previously discussed proposals for medical IRAs and medical savings accounts would also be good interim measures.

2. Decriminalize self-treatment.

You have the right to decide how to deal with your medical problems, who to consult, and what medications to use. This means, for starters, removing legal restrictions on access to medicines. If you want to decide on your own medication, no law should prevent you from buying it directly from a pharmacy, drug company, or health food store. You could consult with a physician for guidance, but you should not need his or her permission (a prescription) for what you choose. This reform would save patients millions in fees now paid for appointments with doctors to get prescriptions.

3. Replace the FDA with private-sector drug testing.

Repeal the FDA's authority to control pharmaceutical testing. The FDA bureaucracy delays for years the availability of proven medication and drives up the cost of all medication. Private-sector testing is well-proven in many fields. Such testing would provide all the information necessary for doctors and patients to make reasonable decisions about what drugs to use for what purposes. Without the FDA's interference, we would have an abundance of safe, high-quality medications at lower prices than we pay today.

4. Replace medical licensing with private-sector certification.

End organized medicine's monopoly on health care. As a first step, state legislatures should license graduates of all medical schools, not just those approved by the AMA. There are many well-trained and experienced physicians from other countries who should be available to those willing to consult them.

Ultimately, state licensing of medical practitioners should end. There are many competent people with healing skills who are not licensed physicians: midwives, nurses, physicians assistants, etc. Medical care is expensive because much of what could be done competently by non-physicians can only be done legally by a licensed physician. Using non-physician professionals would save patients billions. What patients need is information about the training, experience, and qualifications of practitioners so the patient can purchase the appropriate level of counseling or treatment. Currently, private medical boards certify medical specialists. In the absence of government medical licensing, this certification process would expand to cover healing practitioners with various levels of skill and training.

5. Deregulate hospitals.

States typically do not allow the construction or expansion of hospitals unless the proponents prove a "need" for the additional capacity. Medical entrepreneurs who wish to offer hospital services should be allowed to do so. Competition lowers prices when markets are allowed to work in the normal fashion.

6. Bring Medicare and Medicaid to an end.

Since their introduction in 1965, Medicare and Medicaid have done immeasurable damage to health care and cost hundreds of billions in taxes. Many people find it difficult to see how they could survive without these programs, so the greatest obstacle to ending them is political.

The logical first step would be to end Medicaid, as that program is partial federal tax funding for medical welfare programs run by the states. It makes no sense to tax all Americans, siphon off some of the money in Washington, and then send the remainder back to its source in the states.

The states should then end their medical welfare programs, along with all government welfare as discussed in Chapter 12. Medicare is a federal medical welfare program for the elderly, many of whom can afford to pay their medical bills. The first step in phasing out this welfare program would be to remove from its rolls those with financial ability to pay their own bills. Finally, the entire program should end, along with all other current socialist medical schemes.

Individuals deserve to live long, healthy lives. Reducing the government's role in health care and putting more power into the hands of individuals are steps we can take right now to make that possible.

CHAPTER SEVENTEEN

TOWARD A CONSTITUTIONAL FEDERAL GOVERNMENT

Central to libertarian thinking about government is the idea that the people in it have no exemption from the moral code that applies to the rest of us. In other words, the government (and every individual employed by it) should obey the law.

Where the federal government is concerned, it should be bound by the Constitution; it cannot legitimately exercise power in any way not *expressly* and *unequivocally* authorized by the Constitution.

Such a position may appear revolutionary. Today, the courts recognize few constitutional limits on what Congress and the president can do. But the Americans who ratified the Constitution in 1789 would be amazed at today's expansive interpretation of the Constitution. They would be shocked that the federal government has been allowed to legislate virtually all aspects of our lives.

During our lifetimes, the idea that government can, and ought to, solve every problem in society has dominated. No matter what occurs, if someone doesn't like the outcome, the typical reaction is "there ought to be a law." Legislators are always eager to respond. Yet they never ask whether the issue involved is one that legislation can deal with effectively. (It seldom is.) They are even less concerned with whether the legislature *should* deal with the issue.

Are there any aspects of our lives that the federal government must leave alone? It is quite obvious that many politicians in Congress and the executive branch recognize no such limitations. Consider the multitude of federal regulatory agencies and the Federal Register (78,000 pages of federal rules, regulations, presidential proclamations, and executive orders in 2004 alone).

The fact that the Constitution grants certain limited powers to Congress, and that most of what Congress does is manifestly beyond the scope of those limited powers, has been no impediment to politicians' ever-growing urge to control our economic lives.

Nor do Congress and the executive branch restrain from intruding into our personal lives. The most glaring example is the War on Drugs. What could be a more "personal" decision than the choice of what to put into one's body? Where in the Constitution does it say that Congress has the power to pass laws making it a crime for you to ingest any substance? For anyone with a basic grasp of the English language, it is clear that no such power is delineated in the Constitution. There is no constitutional authority for Congress to make any law respecting your health, medications, or *any* substance (chocolate, french fries?) you might choose to ingest.

A SMALL CENTRAL GOVERNMENT WITH LIMITED POWERS

The framers of the Constitution — and the American people who ratified it — were exquisitely sensitive to the risks of creating a federal government. They knew that politicians and government employees inevitably seek to expand their powers. (In 1788, Thomas Jefferson famously warned, "The natural progress of things is for liberty to yield and government to gain ground.")

Supporters of the proposed Constitution argued that it would create a small and relatively weak government with *only* the limited powers that were expressly set forth in the Constitution. But that was not good enough for the people. Before they agreed to ratify the Constitution, they demanded and got a Bill of Rights, listing specific things the federal government was forbidden to do. For example, the Bill of Rights stated that Congress "shall make no law" restricting free speech, curbing freedom of religion, inflicting cruel and unusual punishment, infringing on people's right to "keep and bear arms," and so on.

In opposition, it was argued that a Bill of Rights was not required because the new federal government was granted no power to violate anyone's rights. Government had only those powers clearly listed in the Constitution. Opponents also argued that by listing certain rights that the government could not violate, a Bill of Rights would invite the interpretation that *only* those listed rights were protected. In response to that prescient argument, James Madison proposed the Ninth and Tenth Amendments, which were included in the Bill of Rights.

The Ninth Amendment states, "[t]he enumeration in the Constitution of certain rights shall not be construed to deny or disparage others retained by the people." The Tenth Amendment states, "[t]he powers not delegated to the United States by the Constitution, nor prohibited by it to the States, are reserved to the States respectively or to the people."

The Ninth and Tenth Amendments make it clear that the federal government has *only* those powers expressly granted to it in the Constitution, that the people have many rights in addition to those mentioned in the first eight Amendments, and that all powers not expressly granted to the federal government are retained by the people or the states.

THE "COMMERCE CLAUSE" PATH TO POWER

The Constitution's "Commerce Clause" turned out be to the weak link in the chain designed to restrain the power of the federal government. The Commerce Clause was primarily intended to protect the free flow of trade within the United States. It gave Congress the power to regulate commerce among the states — meaning that Congress could strike down protectionist barriers imposed by state governments. The framers were aware of the negative consequences of restrictions on free trade. They had the experience of European countries and the several years under the Articles of Confederation to teach them, as well as the theoretical foundation provided by Adam Smith's *The Wealth of Nations*.

But instead of being used to expand economic liberty, the Commerce Clause was used to expand the power of the federal government to regulate almost anything — whether or not it actually involved interstate commerce. In one of its most famous (and destructive) rulings, the Supreme Court held in 1942 (*Wickard v. Filburn*) that the federal government could regulate the amount of wheat grown by a farmer. The Ohio farmer in question planted a few acres to feed his family and his livestock. He did not intend to sell the wheat across state lines.

However, in an astonishing display of convoluted logic, the Supreme Court unanimously ruled that if the farmer grew wheat for personal use, then he would not purchase wheat from others. Thus, his home-grown wheat "competes with wheat in commerce," the justices wrote. The ruling established the doctrine that a product with nothing to do with interstate commerce could still theoretically *affect* interstate commerce, thus bringing it under the control of the federal government.

To anyone aware of the context of the Constitution's adoption, it's obvious that the ruling was a disaster. The Commerce Clause was never intended to give the federal government the power to control any activity that might have some distant effect on commerce between people in more than one state.

In fact, if that is what the Commerce Clause *does* mean, then the Constitution is not a grant of clear and limited powers at all. Because all human activity has *some* connection (however tenuous) to commerce, and because all commerce has *some* impact (however tenuous) on commerce between states, that interpretation of the Commerce Clause means the federal government's power to regulate everything and everybody is unlimited. To accept the unlimited power view of the Commerce Clause is to say that the Ninth and Tenth Amendments must be ignored, as if they had never existed.

NATURAL RIGHTS: KEY TO CONSTITUTIONAL INTERPRETATION

How should the Constitution be interpreted? What are the proper constitutional limits on what the federal government can do? One answer is provided by the natural rights theory expressed in the Declaration of Independence. Government exists only for the limited purpose of protecting the rights of the citizens. Each person has rights equal to each other person. No person, including those in government, has the right to trample the rights of another, no matter how much good he might think it would do. Government has no legitimate power to act as Nanny to protect us from making potentially stupid decisions in what we buy, use or ingest, or how we choose to live our lives.

Or, as Jefferson put it in his first Inaugural Address, "[A] wise and frugal government, which shall restrain men from injuring one another, which shall leave them otherwise free to regulate their own pursuits of industry and improvement, and shall not take from the mouth of labor the bread it has earned. This is the sum of good government...."

Anyone who values liberty — and anyone who wants human beings to flourish in conditions of peace and abundance — must begin by rejecting the view that the federal government has unlimited power. They must reject the view that it is morally appropriate for the federal government to play a role in every situation that may displease some among us.

Rather, we should always raise the questions consistent with America's natural rights tradition. Where in the Constitution does it say that the federal government has the power to do that? Did we the people give our consent to be governed in this way?

Let us place the burden of proof on the advocates of expanded government power. Let us demand that they point to the language in the Constitution that *specifically* authorizes the legislation or regulation that they seek to impose on us. Let us insist that they explain why any proposed government intervention is consistent with the limited-government vision articulated by the Founding Fathers.

PROPERLY LIMITED FEDERAL GOVERNMENT

In my view, the federal government has only two legitimate functions. The first is national defense. The second is to protect our constitutional rights from violations by state and local governments. A good historical example of the latter is the federal elimination of the Jim Crow laws in Southern states. Such laws denied African-Americans equal protection of the law to which they are entitled under the Fourteenth Amendment.

Until we reach that state of affairs, we can aim at a more modest reform: limiting the federal government to only those powers and functions expressly stated in the Constitution. In other words, make the federal government obey the law.

What might such a federal government look like? The easy answer is to list a few of the many federal departments and agencies that are *not* authorized by the Constitution. None would remain in a constitutional federal government:

1. Department of Energy
2. Department of Education
3. Department of Labor
4. Department of Agriculture
5. Department of Commerce
6. Department of Transportation
7. Department of Health and Human Services
8. Drug Enforcement Administration
9. Bureau of Alcohol, Tobacco and Firearms
10. Federal Aviation Administration
11. Federal Communications Commission
12. Federal Trade Commission
13. Environmental Protection Agency
14. Federal Emergency Management Agency
15. Equal Employment Opportunities Commission
16. Tennessee Valley Authority
17. Amtrak

You get the picture. Eliminating the departments and agencies on that list would be a partial, but valuable, step in the right direction. A genuinely constitutional federal government would be a fraction of its current size and would cost a fraction of the $2.4 trillion annual budgets we have come to expect from politicians in power.

Cutting the federal government back to its proper constitutional dimensions will mean that the federal government will have to follow the law (just like you and me). It also means that hundreds of billions of dollars annually will no longer be taken from those who earn it and delivered to Washington politicians — who then spread it around for the purpose of keeping themselves in power. Instead, those hard-earned dollars will remain with individuals, who can use their own money to improve their lives and their family's lives according to their own values.

CHAPTER EIGHTEEN

COMPARING LIBERAL, CONSERVATIVE, AND LIBERTARIAN ANSWERS

Here are some frequently asked questions about political issues. Each question is followed by a short, typical response from a liberal, a conservative, and a libertarian.

Because all liberals and conservatives do not think alike, the responses listed for them are naturally subject to challenge. However, I've tried to be fair — and to accurately represent what *most* liberals or conservatives might say. These responses are based on conversations I've had with hundreds of people who described themselves as liberals or conservatives, and on the published writings of self-described liberals and conservatives. The libertarian responses are based upon my views and the writings of libertarian scholars.

Obviously, these quick answers offer just an overview of libertarian thinking. Some of these issues are discussed at greater length in various chapters of this book. Other issues have been extensively addressed by libertarian scholars and think tanks. I encourage you to do additional reading if the libertarian position seems surprising, or if you don't think it would work in the "real world." In every case, you'll find that libertarian policies are practical, realistic, and already in effect in some part of the United States or the world.

■ *Should there be a draft for military purposes?*
Liberal: Yes, but not during peacetime.

Conservative: Yes. America must always be strong to deter potential enemies. And young people need military service to learn patriotism and discipline.

Libertarian: Absolutely not, under any circumstances. The draft is slavery. Slaves make poor defenders of freedom.

■ *Should government own or control newspapers, radio, or television?*

Liberal: Yes. We need the Public Broadcasting System (PBS) to guarantee high-quality programming. In addition, the government should restrict advertising aimed at children. We also need laws to ensure balanced coverage by the conservative-dominated talk radio networks.

Conservative: Government should not own radio or TV networks but should make it a crime for them to broadcast offensive material. We also need laws to ensure balanced coverage by the liberal-dominated television networks.

Libertarian: No. Government ownership or control of press or electronic media has no place in a free society. Owners of newspapers and broadcasters should be responsible for what they publish. Let parents and consumers decide what may come into their homes.

■ *Should government regulate sexual activity among consenting adults, including prostitution?*

Liberal: Generally not. But if prostitution were legal, it should be regulated to protect public health and to make sure that women are not exploited.

Conservative: Yes. Prostitution, homosexuality, adultery, and fornication should all be illegal because they are antithetical to family and religious values.

Libertarian: No. Sexual activity involving consenting adults violates the rights of no other person. The right of adults to make their own decisions in this most private area must be respected.

■ *Should drugs like marijuana, cocaine, and heroin be legalized?*

Liberal: Perhaps. Marijuana could be legalized, but the production and sale should be regulated and taxed. Tax money should be used for drug-treatment programs.

Conservative: Are you nuts? Drugs cause crime, harm families, encourage criminal gangs, and promote other social ills. We need stricter anti-drug laws, longer sentences, and more prisons.

Libertarian: Yes. Peaceful drug use violates no other person's rights. People have the right to control their own bodies. Drug laws subsidize criminals, cause more crime, corrupt law enforcement, destroy civil liberties, and do not work.

■ *Should it be legal for people to travel or move into and out of the U.S. without limitation?*

Liberal: We should allow people trying to escape political oppression to come to America, and give them government aid to help them get settled. But we should strictly limit their number because they take American jobs.

Conservative: No. We have too many immigrants already. They go on welfare, take our jobs, increase crime and disease, and refuse to learn English.

Libertarian: Yes. All individuals have the same rights, regardless of where they were born. Anyone willing to take responsibility for himself or herself has the right to travel and seek opportunity. America has always benefitted from immigrants. They tend to work hard, start businesses, become educated, improve our economy, and make America a more culturally dynamic place.

■ *Should government subsidize farmers and regulate what they grow?*

Liberal: Yes. Farmers need protection from low prices for their crops and against bad weather. Also, these farm programs help supply food to the needy.

Conservative: Some support is needed so that family farms are not lost, and to protect American farmers against unfair foreign competition. Many farm programs are expensive and wasteful, but they can't be completely eliminated.

Libertarian: No. Businesses are not entitled to have the government force taxpayers to support them. Farmers should operate in a free, competitive market, just as all others in business should.

■ *Should government impose tariffs, quotas, embargoes, or other restrictions on international trade?*

Liberal: Yes. Tariffs and quotas are needed to save American jobs. Trade embargoes can also be used to punish right-wing dictators who oppress their people.

Conservative: Yes. Trade barriers are necessary to protect industries vital to national defense and to keep American businesses competitive. Trade embargoes can also be used to punish left-wing dictators who oppress their people.

Libertarian: No. Trade barriers violate the rights of Americans and foreign people who desire to trade. Trade barriers cut everyone's productivity and cost more jobs than they save.

■ *Should the government mandate a minimum wage?*

Liberal: Yes. Otherwise, employers will exploit workers by paying only subsistence wages. Everyone is entitled to a living wage.

Conservative: No. Employers should be able to hire the best employees they can get at the lowest price set by market competition.

Libertarian: No. Such laws violate the right of employees and employers to strike their own deals. Economics and history show that minimum wage laws increase unemployment.

■ *Isn't taxation the only way to pay for necessary government services?*

Liberal: Without taxes, not enough people would be willing to pay for welfare for the poor, or education, or environmental protection, or so many other important things which only government can provide. In fact, the government should probably raise taxes so it can do more good.

Conservative: Without taxes, not enough people would be willing to pay for a national defense, or subsidies to vital industries, or to fight the War on Drugs, or so many other important things only government can provide. However, taxes are somewhat high, so it may be possible to reduce them slightly.

Libertarian: Taxation is immoral and indistinguishable from theft. We should replace taxation with voluntary methods of funding legitimate government functions. Besides, most "government services" can be provided by private-sector businesses, charities, and other organizations.

■ *Should the U.S. government send troops to intervene in the affairs of other countries?*

Liberal: Yes, if it will advance the cause of human rights, topple oppressive right-wing dictators, or help poor and starving people in Third-World countries.

Conservative: Yes, if it will help fight terrorism, topple oppressive left-wing dictators, or protect vital U.S. interests such as oil.

Libertarian: No. The U.S. government has no authority to intervene militarily in the affairs of other countries except in response to a military attack on the American homeland.

■ *Should the United States government continue to participate in and support the United Nations?*

Liberal: Yes, because the U.N. is the last best hope for world peace and because it performs valuable humanitarian missions.

Conservative: Yes, but we should pressure the U.N. to take more pro-American stances.

Libertarian: Not as presently constituted and financed by tax dollars. A voluntarily financed forum for international cooperation would not be objectionable.

■ *Should young Americans be compelled to serve in some capacity in the name of "national service"?*

Liberal: Yes, everyone has the obligation to "give back" for what society has done for them, and to learn the importance of helping others.

Conservative: Yes, when it can be justified for national defense purposes.

Libertarian: No. Mandatory labor is slavery regardless of whether it is masked by the euphemisms "draft" or "national service."

■ *Should the U.S. government help American businesses during hard economic times with low-interest loans or subsidies?*

Liberal: Yes. This will save jobs, and American workers need all the help they can get during a recession. However, corporations shouldn't be allowed to use such support to make excessive profits.

Conservative: Yes. Government should help business stay in business. Such a policy promotes free enterprise.

Libertarian: No. Government can only help some businesses by stealing from other businesses and taxpayers. No one has the right to be subsidized at the expense of others.

■ *What is the best way to deal with the current massive budget deficits?*

Liberal: Raise taxes on the rich. Don't cut federal spending on social programs.

Conservative: In the short term, borrow more money to keep the federal government operating. Don't raise taxes, and don't cut federal spending on defense. In the long run, economic growth will help pay down the national debt.

Libertarian: Dramatically reduce federal spending and taxes to encourage greater economic growth. Confine the federal government to national defense and protecting our constitutional rights. With those savings, pay down the national debt as quickly as possible.

■ *Is there a solution to the long-term financial problems of the Social Security system?*

Liberal: Significantly increase payroll taxes. Older people are entitled to live in dignity, and they need the security of a government-financed retirement program.

Conservative: Reduce benefits, make the system more efficient, and raise the retirement age. Also, consider implementing voluntary, government-controlled private retirement accounts with a portion of people's Social Security taxes. If necessary, borrow more money to keep the system afloat.

Libertarian: The impending Social Security bankruptcy requires that we end the system by granting older workers and retirees the choice of a lump-sum payment or private insurance annuity to replace future Social Security benefits. Ending the bankrupt system will relieve younger workers of the tax and avoid the economic meltdown which will surely result from a massive increase in Social Security taxes.

■ *Should the U.S. government send foreign aid to other countries?*
Liberal: Yes. We need to help the poor in Third-World and developing countries which have good human-rights records.
Conservative: Yes. We need to help those governments trying to resist terrorism or trying to convert from socialism to democracy.
Libertarian: No. American taxpayers should not be forced to pay to support other governments. However, individuals should always be allowed to give voluntary aid.

■ *Should children be required by law to attend schools?*
Liberal: Yes. Parents cannot be trusted to provide for their children's education.
Conservative: Yes. Education is too important to the economic health of the nation to be left up to parents.
Libertarian: No. Compulsory attendance laws violate the rights of parents to decide what kind of education is best for their children.

■ *Should parents be allowed to teach their children at home?*
Liberal: Maybe. However, it should be strictly regulated to make sure that parents don't teach their children bigotry or bizarre religious doctrines.
Conservative: Yes. Although some parents may fail to give their children a proper education, public schools aren't doing a very good job. However, increased federal oversight of schools and standardized testing may solve that problem, which will encourage homeschoolers to return to the public-education system.
Libertarian: Yes. The government has no proper role in education. There should be a separation of *school* and state for the same reasons that we have a separation of church and state. There should be no government penalties or regulation of parents who prefer to teach their children at home.

■ *Should the ownership of firearms be restricted by law?*

Liberal: Yes. Guns kill people. Ownership of firearms should be very strictly regulated, with waiting periods, mandatory gun locks, background checks, and government-issued licenses. If those steps don't solve the problem, then only law enforcement and the military should be allowed to own any type of gun.

Conservative: Generally, no. However, some limitations on hand guns and military assault rifles may be appropriate.

Libertarian: No. Ownership of firearms violates no other person's rights, and therefore should not be subject to any penalty or government restriction. Aggressive (criminal) use of firearms should be punished, but not responsible ownership.

■ *What should the government do about the rising cost of health care?*

Liberal: Every American has a right to health care. The federal government should guarantee free health care, or at least insurance, for everyone. Government must control fees charged by greedy doctors, hospitals, HMOs, and pharmaceutical companies.

Conservative: Medicare entitlements must be controlled and limits should be put on medical malpractice lawsuits. Business and individuals should get more tax breaks for medical expenses.

Libertarian: Eliminate the socialist policies that drive up costs. End the government-enforced doctor's monopoly. Let midwives, nurses, and other professionals provide medical service. Give patients the power to make more medical decisions. Deregulate hospitals and insurance. Replace Medicare with voluntary private funding for the needy. As a transition step, offer dollar-for-dollar tax breaks for all medical costs.

■ *What should government policy be toward abortion?*

Liberal: A woman has the right to an abortion. If she can't afford it, taxpayers should pay for her abortion.

Conservative: Abortion is murder and should be subject to appropriate criminal penalties (except, perhaps, in the case of rape or incest).

Libertarian: This is a rare issue where libertarians can disagree.

Most libertarians hold that a woman has the right to decide whether to terminate a pregnancy, and that government should play no role in that decision. Other libertarians hold that abortion involves a violation of the rights of an unborn child, and should be illegal. All libertarians agree that under no circumstances should government force anyone to subsidize another's abortion.

■ *What should government policy be toward nuclear power?*

Liberal: Because of high risk and the problem of nuclear waste disposal, no more nuclear power plants should be built and existing plants should be shut down.

Conservative: Nuclear power is cheap, safe, and less polluting than other power sources. Government should do more to encourage its development.

Libertarian: The nuclear power industry is subsidized by federally legislated limits on liability. Government should get out of the nuclear power business and let private power companies compete in the energy marketplace — while bearing full responsibility for actual or potential liability.

■ *Do we need the Food and Drug Administration to ensure that medicines are safe and effective?*

Liberal: Yes. Only government can protect us against events like the Thalidomide tragedy (when a drug turned out to have unanticipated side effects). But we do need to speed up the FDA approval process for diseases like AIDS.

Conservative: Yes. But the FDA needs to be reformed. Currently, the approval process is so slow and expensive that it discourages pharmaceutical companies from developing new drugs.

Libertarian: No. There is a market demand for information about the safety and effectiveness of medicine. That demand can be met by private testing labs, the same way Underwriters Laboratories tests and reports on electrical appliances. The FDA causes delays in the approval of medicines that lead to unnecessary deaths and suffering by people denied medicine for extended periods.

■ *Do we need zoning laws to protect our communities?*

Liberal: Yes. Zoning is necessary to control sprawl, to protect open spaces, and to guarantee sufficient low-income housing. It's also needed to make sure that profit-hungry businesses like WalMart can't build "big-box" stores wherever they want.

Conservative: Yes. Zoning is necessary to ensure stable property values, to protect historic neighborhoods, and to maintain the quality of life we want in our communities.

Libertarian: No. Zoning denies the right of individuals to make the best use of their property. Experience in unzoned cities like Houston proves that cities can thrive without zoning. Rents are lower, property values are protected, and compatible uses tend to cluster together. Other free-market alternatives are things like private deed restrictions or covenants.

■ *Do we need the federal Small Business Administration (SBA) to provide loans to entrepreneurs and small business?*

Liberal: Yes. Otherwise many minority-run or female-owned businesses would not be able to get start-up funds and create jobs in their communities.

Conservative: Yes. Anything that helps free enterprise is a good thing.

Libertarian: No. The SBA is just another example of welfare for business. The agency hands out money that was seized from working taxpayers and successful businesses. It gives that money to people who failed to persuade lenders to loan them funds voluntarily. Free-market venture capitalists are perfectly capable of deciding which new businesses have a realistic chance of succeeding, and lending money accordingly.

CONCLUSION

The libertarian movement includes millions of individuals and a multitude of organizations. All of them share a fundamental commitment to certain ethical and political ideas that are the foundation for America's great experiment in tolerance and liberty. It is a movement respectful of individual differences; it values personal responsibility; it values cooperation over coercion; it values independent thought and private decision making; and it values learning from experience to guide the future.

Libertarians cherish the American heritage of liberty, personal responsibility, and respect for the rights of others. Those ideas made it possible for Americans to build a society of abundance and opportunity for anyone willing to make the effort. Libertarians recognize the responsibility we all share to preserve this precious heritage for our children and grandchildren.

Libertarians believe that you deserve to live a free and independent life. We want a system which encourages all people to choose what they want from life; a system that lets them live, love, work, play, and dream their own way, at their own pace, however they wish and with whom they wish, accepting whatever consequences come.

The libertarian way is a caring, people-centered approach to politics. We believe each individual is unique. We want a system which respects each special individual and encourages all of us to discover the best within ourselves. We want a system that allows all of us to realize our full potential; a system that encourages and rewards harmonious relationships among all people.

The libertarian way is a logically consistent approach to politics based on the moral principle of self-ownership. All libertarian positions on political issues are consistent with the idea that each individual has the right to control his or her own body, action, speech, and property. Accordingly, government's only proper role is to assist individuals when they need to defend themselves and their rights.

Surely, these libertarian values are shared, in some substantial measure, by people of good will everywhere.

The libertarian movement, international in scope, is composed of all the individuals who consciously share and are working to promote these libertarian ideals and values.

Our libertarian vision has growing appeal. Hundreds of millions of people show daily by their actions that they agree with libertarian ideals of tolerance and harmony. These millions live their lives accordingly, respecting the rights of others in virtually everything they do. As totalitarian governments collapse around the world, people increasingly demand liberty, free markets, and political systems which respect them as sovereign individuals. When given the choice, most people prefer the libertarian way. Not Utopia — just liberty and the opportunities it brings.

In the foregoing chapters we have seen something of the history of the development of libertarianism as a uniquely American political philosophy. Although its roots are in the centuries-old natural rights tradition, it took the American Revolution to translate libertarianism into practical political action — with magnificent success — for the first time in history. The modern libertarian movement is a continuation of that first libertarian revolution.

If this book is your first introduction to libertarianism, it's likely you have many questions. That's not surprising. I'm well aware that what has been said here contradicts much of what most Americans have learned in history or political science classes. For that reason, an extensive bibliography is included. It suggests additional readings on many of the subjects this book could only briefly address. Most of the books listed in the *Suggested Reading* section can be obtained from Laissez Faire Books, which can be found online at www.laissezfairebooks.com.

SUGGESTED READING

AN INTRODUCTORY SELECTION

David Boaz, *Libertarianism: A Primer* (New York: The Free Press, 1997)

Harry Browne, *Why Government Doesn't Work* (New York: St. Martin's Press, 1995)

Milton and Rose Friedman, *Free to Choose* (New York: Avon Books, 1979, 1980)

Henry Hazlitt, *Economics In One Lesson* (Westport, Conn.: Arlington House, 1946, 1962, 1979)

Tibor R. Machan, Ed, *The Libertarian Reader* (Totowa, NJ: Rowman and Littlefield, 1982)

Charles Murray, *What It Means To Be A Libertarian: A Personal Interpretation* (New York: Broadway Books, 1997)

Ayn Rand, *Atlas Shrugged* (New York: Random House, 1957)

Mary J. Ruwart, *Healing Our World In an Age of Aggression* (Kalamazoo, Mich.: Sun Star Press, 2003)

FOREIGN POLICY AND NATIONAL DEFENSE

Stephen E. Ambrose, *Rise to Globalism: American Foreign Policy Since 1938* (New York: Penguin Books, 1985)

John V. Denson, Ed., *The Costs of War: America's Pyrrhic Victories* (New Brunswick: Transaction Publishers, 1999)

Thomas Fleming, *The Illusion of Victory: America in World War I* (New York: Basic Books, 2003)

Thomas Fleming, *The New Dealers' War: FDR and the War Within World War II* (New York: Basic Books, 2001)

Chalmers Johnson, *The Sorrows of Empire: Militarism, Secrecy, and the End of the Republic* (New York: Henry Holt, 2004)

Jonathon Kwitny, *Endless Enemies: The Making of an Unfriendly World* (New York: Congdon & Weed, Inc., 1984)

Seymour Melman, *The Permanent War Economy* (New York: Touchstone, 1974, 1985)

ECONOMICS, ECONOMIC HISTORY, AND POLICY

Frederic Bastiat, *Economic Sophisms* (Princeton, NJ: Van Nostrand, 1964)

James A. Dorn and Henry G. Manne, Ed., *Economic Liberties and the Judiciary* (Fairfax, Virginia: George Mason University Press, 1987)

David Friedman, *Hidden Order: The Economics of Everyday Life* (New York: Harper Business, 1996)

Friedrich A. Hayek, *Denationalization of Money* (London: Institute of Economic Affairs, 1978)

Ludwig von Mises, *Human Action* (New Haven: Yale University Press, 1949; Auburn, Alabama: Ludwig von Mises Institute, 1998)

Ludwig von Mises, *Socialism* (New Haven: Yale University Press, 1951, 1959, 1962)

Nathan Rosenberg and L.P. Birdzell, *How the West Grew Rich: Economic Transformation of the Industrial World* (New York: Basic Books, 1984)

Murray N. Rothbard, *Man, Economy and State* (Princeton: Van Nostrand, 1962; Auburn, Alabama: Ludwig von Mises Institute, 2004)

POLITICAL PHILOSOPHY

Doug Bandow, *The Politics of Envy: Statism as Theology* (New Brunswick: Transaction Publishers, 1994)

Etienne de la Boetie, *Politics of Obedience: The Discourse Of Voluntary Servitude* (New York: Free Life Editions, 1975)

Georgia Law Review, Articles — Perspectives on Rights (University of Georgia, School of Law, Summer 1979)

Friedrich A. Hayek, *The Fatal Conceit* (Chicago: University of Chicago Press, 1988)

Friedrich A. Hayek, *The Road To Serfdom* (Chicago: University of Chicago Press, 1944, 1972)

Auberon Herbert, *The Right and Wrong of Compulsion by the State* (Indianapolis: Liberty Fund, 1978)

Robert Higgs, *Against Leviathan: Government Policy and a Free Society* (Oakland, Calif.: The Independent Institute, 2004)

Hans-Herman Hoppe, *Democracy, The God That Failed: The Economics and Politics of Monarchy, Democracy, and Natural Order* (New Brunswick: Transaction Publishers, 2001)

Anthony de Jasay, *Against Politics: On Government, Anarchy and Order* (New York and London: Rutledge, 1997)

Ludwig von Mises, *Omnipotent Government: The Rise of the Total State and Total War* (New Rochelle, NY: Arlington House, 1969)

Franz Oppenheimer, *The State* (New York: Free Life Editions, 1914, 1942, 1975)

Ayn Rand, *Capitalism: The Unknown Ideal* (New York: Signet, 1987)

Helmut Schoeck, *Envy: A Theory of Social Behavior* (New York: Harcourt, Brace & World, Inc., 1969)

SOCIAL POLICY

Doug Bandow, *The Politics of Plunder: Misgovernment in Washington* (New Brunswick: Transaction Publishers, 1990)

Bruce L. Benson, *To Serve and Protect: Privatization and Community in Criminal Justice* (New York: New York University Press, 1998)

James Bovard, *The Farm Fiasco* (San Francisco: ICS Press, 1989)

Williamson M. Evers, Ed., *National Service: Pro and Con* (Stanford: Hoover Institution Press, 1990)

Peter J. Ferrara, Ed., *Free the Mail: Ending the Postal Monopoly* (Washington, DC: Cato Institute, 1990)

Nat Hentoff, *The First Freedom* (New York: Dell, 1980)

Charles Murray, *In Pursuit of Happiness and Good Government* (New York: Simon & Schuster, 1988)

Julian L. Simon, *The Ultimate Resource 2* (Princeton: Princeton University Press, 1996)

Walter E. Williams, *The State Against Blacks* (New York: McGraw-Hill, 1982)

TAXATION, TAX POLICY, AND THE IRS

Charles Adams, *For Good and Evil: The Impact of Taxes on the Course of Civilization* (New York: Madison Books, 1993)

David Burnham, *A Law Unto Itself: The IRS And The Abuse Of Power* (New York: Vintage Books, 1989)

George Hansen, *To Harass Our People: The IRS and Government Abuse of Power* (Washington, DC: Positive Publications, 1984)

James L. Payne, *Costly Returns: The Burdens of the U.S. Tax System* (San Francisco: Institute for Contemporary Studies, 1993)

SOCIAL SECURITY

Abraham Ellis, *The Social Security Fraud* (New York: Foundation for Economic Education, 1996)

Peter J. Ferrara, *Social Security: Averting the Crisis* (Washington, DC: Cato Institute, 1982)

Peter J. Ferrara, *Social Security: Prospects for Real Reform* (Washington, DC: Cato Institute, 1985)

James Turk, *Social Security: Lies, Myths and Reality* (Greenwich, Conn.: Greenfield Books, 1992)

GUN RIGHTS AND THE SECOND AMENDMENT

Clayton E. Cramer, *For the Defense of Themselves and the State* (Westport, Conn.: Praeger, 1994)

Stephen P. Halbrook, *That Every Man Be Armed* (Oakland, Calif.: The Independent Institute, 1994)

Don B. Kates and Gary Kleck, *The Great American Gun Debate* (San Francisco: Pacific Research Institute, 1997)

Don B. Kates, Jr., Ed., *Firearms and Violence* (San Francisco: Pacific Institute For Public Policy Research, 1984)

David Kopel, *The Samurai, the Mountie, and the Cowboy: Should America Adopt the Gun Controls of Other Democracies?* (Buffalo, NY: Prometheus Books, 1992)

John R. Lott, Jr., *The Bias Against Guns: Why Almost Everything You've Heard About Gun Control Is Wrong* (Washington, DC: Regnery, 2003)

John R. Lott, Jr., *More Guns, Less Crime: Understanding Crime and Gun Control Laws* (Chicago: University of Chicago Press, 1998)

Wayne LaPierre, *Guns, Crime and Freedom* (Washington, DC: Regnery, 1994)

Richard Poe, *The Seven Myths of Gun Control: Reclaiming the Truth About Guns, Crime, and the Second Amendment* (Roseville, Calif.: Prima Publishing, 2001)

WELFARE AND "CIVIL RIGHTS"

W. Michael Cox and Richard Alm, *Myths of Rich and Poor: Why We're Better Off Than We Think* (New York: Basic Books, 1999)

Richard A. Epstein, *Forbidden Grounds: The Case Against Employment Discrimination Laws* (Cambridge: Harvard University Press, 1992)

Charles Murray, *Losing Ground: American Social Policy 1950-1980* (New York: Basic Books, 1984)

Marvin Olasky, *The Tragedy of American Compassion* (Washington, DC: Regnery Gateway, 1992)

Thomas Sowell, *Civil Rights: Rhetoric or Reality* (New York: Wm. Morrow & Co., Inc., 1984)

Michael Tanner, *The End of Welfare* (Washington, DC: Cato Institute, 1996)

DRUGS AND DRUG POLICY

David Boaz, Ed., *The Crisis of Drug Prohibition* (Washington, DC: Cato Institute, 1990)

Edward M. Brecher and *Consumer Reports*, Ed., *Licit & Illicit Drugs* (Boston and Toronto: Little, Brown, 1972)

Milton Friedman and Thomas S. Szasz, *On Liberty and Drugs* (Washington, DC: The Drug Policy Foundation Press, 1992)

Peter McWilliams, *Ain't Nobody's Business If You Do: The Absurdity of Consensual Crimes in Our Free Country* (Los Angeles: Prelude Press, 1996)

Jeffrey A. Miron, *Drug War Crimes: The Consequences of Prohibition* (Oakland, Calif.: The Independent Institute, 2004)

David W. Rasmussen and Bruce L. Benson, *The Economic Anatomy of a Drug War* (Lanham, Maryland: Rowman & Littlefield, 1994)

Sam Staley, *Drug Policy and the Decline of American Cities* (New Brunswick: Transaction Publishers, 1992)

Arnold S. Trebach, *The Heroin Solution* (New Haven: Yale University Press, 1982)

Thomas Szasz, *Ceremonial Chemistry: The Ritual Persecution of Drugs, Addicts and Pushers* (Holmes Beach, Florida: Learning Publications, 1985)

Steven Wisotsky, *Beyond the War on Drugs: Overcoming a Failed Public Policy* (Buffalo: Prometheus Books, 1990)

HEALTH CARE

Joseph L. Bast, Richard C. Rue & Stuart A. Wesbury, Jr., *Why We Spend Too Much on Health Care* (Chicago: The Heartland Institute, 1992)

John C. Goodman, *The Regulation of Medical Care: Is the Price Too High?* (Washington, DC: Cato Institute, 1980)

John C. Goodman & Gerald L Musgrave, *Patient Power: Solving America's Health Care Crisis* (Washington, DC: Cato Institute, 1992)

Terree P. Wasley, *What Has Government Done to Our Health Care?* (Washington, DC: Cato Institute, 1992)

CIVIL LIBERTIES UNDER ATTACK

David E. Bernstein, *You Can't Say That: The Growing Threat to Civil Liberties From Antidiscrimination Laws* (Washington, DC: Cato Institute, 2003)

James Bovard, *Feeling Your Pain: The Explosion and Abuse of Government Power in the Clinton-Gore Years* (New York: St. Martin's Press, 2000)

James Bovard, *Freedom in Chains: The Rise of the State and the Demise of the Citizen* (New York: St. Martin's Press, 1999)

James Bovard, *Lost Rights: The Destruction of American Liberty* (New York: St. Martin's Press, 1994)

Frank J. Donner, *The Age of Surveillance* (New York: Vintage Books, 1981)

Gene Healy, Ed., *Go Directly to Jail: The Criminalization of Almost Everything* (Washington, DC: Cato Institute, 2004)

David Wise, *The American Police State: The Government Against the People* (New York: Random House, 1976)

EDUCATION AND EDUCATIONAL POLICY

David and Micki Colfax, *Homeschooling for Excellence* (New York: Warner Books, 1988)

Andrew J. Coulson, *Market Education: The Unknown History* (New Brunswick: Social Policy and Philosophy Center, 1999)

John Taylor Gatto, Ed., *The Exhausted School* (New York: The Oxford Village Press, 1993)

David Guterson, *Family Matters: Why Homeschooling Makes Sense* (New York: Harcourt Brace, 1992)

Grace Llewellyn, *The Teenage Liberation Handbook: How to Quit School and Get a Real Life and Education* (Eugene, Oregon: Lowry House, 1991)

Myron Lieberman, *Privatization and Educational Choice* (New York: St. Martin's Press, 1989)

Myron Lieberman, *Public Education: An Autopsy* (Cambridge: Harvard University Press, 1993)

Sheldon Richman, *Separating School and State: How to Liberate America's Families* (Fairfax, Virginia: Future of Freedom Foundation, 1994)

LAW AND LEGAL HISTORY

Randy E. Barnet, *Restoring the Lost Constitution: The Presumption of Liberty* (Princeton: Princeton University Press, 2004)

Randy E. Barnett, Ed., *The Rights Retained by the People: The History and Meaning of the Ninth Amendment* (Fairfax, Virginia: George Mason University Press, 1989)

Richard A. Epstein, *Takings: Private Property and the Power of Eminent Domain* (Cambridge: Harvard University Press, 1984)

Peter W. Huber, *Liability: The Legal Revolution and Its Consequences* (New York: Basic Books, 1988)

Bruno Leoni, *Freedom and the Law* (Indianapolis: Liberty Fund, 1961, 1972, 1991)

Friedrich A. Hayek, *Law, Legislation and Liberty* [3 Volumes] (Chicago: University of Chicago Press, 1979)

Bernard H. Seigan, *Property and Freedom: The Constitution, the Courts, and Land-Use Regulation* (New Brunswick: Transaction Publishers, 1997)

THE ENVIRONMENT

John Baden, Ed., *Environmental Gore: A Constructive Response to Earth in the Balance* (San Francisco: Pacific Research Institute for Public Policy, 1994)

John Baden and Richard L. Stroup, Ed., *Natural Resources: Bureaucratic Myths and Environmental Management* (San Francisco: Pacific Institute for Public Policy Research, 1983)

John Baden and Richard L. Stroup, Ed., *Bureaucracy v. Environment: The Environmental Cost of Bureaucratic Governance* (Ann Arbor: University of Michigan Press, 1981)

Joseph L. Bast, Peter J. Hill and Richard C. Rue, *Eco-Sanity: A Common-Sense Guide to Environmentalism* (Lanham, Maryland: Madison Books, 1994)

Wilfred Beckerman, *Through Green-Colored Glasses: Environmentalism Reconsidered* (Washington, DC: Cato Institute, 1996)

Wallace Kaufman, *No Turning Back: Dismantling the Fantasies of Environmental Thinking* (New York: Basic Books, 1994)

Michael Sanera and Jane S. Shaw, *Facts Not Fear: A Parent's Guide to Teaching Children About the Environment* (Washington, DC: Regnery, 1996)

Julian Simon, *Hoodwinking the Nation* (New Brunswick: Transaction Publishers, 1999)

Julian Simon, *Population Matters: People, Resources, Environment and Immigration* (New Brunswick: Transaction Publishers, 1990)

Julian Simon and Herman Kahn, *The Resourceful Earth: A Response to Global 2000* (New York and Oxford: Basil Blackwell, 1984)

PERSPECTIVES ON THE WORLD AND PEOPLE

Robert Conquest, *Harvest Of Sorrow: Soviet Collectivization and the Terror Famine* (New York: Oxford University Press, 1986)

Paul Johnson, *Modern Times: The World From the Twenties to the Eighties* (New York: Harper & Row, 1983)

R.J. Rummel, *Death By Government* (New Brunswick: Transaction Publishers 1994)

Alexander Rustow, *Freedom and Domination: A Historical Critique of Civilization* (Princeton: Princeton University Press, 1980)

Thomas Sowell, *A Conflict of Visions: Ideological Origins of Political Struggles* (New York: William Morrow, 1987)

Thomas Sowell, *Conquests and Cultures: An International History* (New York: Basic Books, 1998)

Thomas Sowell, *Migrations and Cultures: A World View* (New York: Basic Books, 1996)

Thomas Sowell, *Race and Culture: A World View* (New York: Basic Books, 1994)

AMERICA AND AMERICAN HISTORY

Bernard Bailyn, *The Ideological Origins of the American Revolution* (Cambridge, Mass.: Belknap Press, 1967)

Thomas J. DiLorenzo, *The Real Lincoln* (New York: Three Rivers Press, 2003)

Frederick Douglass, *My Bondage and My Freedom* (New York: Dover Publications, Inc., 1855, 1969)

Robert Higgs, *Crisis and Leviathan: Critical Episodes in the Growth of American Government* (New York: Oxford University Press, 1987)

Jeffrey Rogers Hummel, *Emancipating Slaves, Enslaving Free Men* (Chicago: Open Court, 1996)

Jackson Turner Main, *The Anti-Federalists: Critics of the Constitution 1781-1788* (New York: W.W. Norton, 1961)

Murray N. Rothbard, *Conceived In Liberty* [4 Vols.] (San Francisco: Cobden Press, 1979)

Thomas Sowell, *Ethnic America* (New York: Basic Books, 1981)

Lysander Spooner, *No Treason: The Constitution of No Authority*

(Colorado Springs: Ralph Miles Publisher, Inc., 1973)

Alexis de Tocqueville, *Democracy In America* (Garden City, NY: Anchor Books, 1969)

Thomas E. Woods, Jr., *The Politically Incorrect Guide to American History* (Washington, DC: Regnery, 2004)

LIBERTARIAN ORGANIZATIONS

The libertarian movement is vast, fast-growing, and worldwide in scope. There are hundreds of organizations that are libertarian, libertarian-leaning, or advocate libertarian solutions on a specific issue. The list continues to grow almost daily.

There are think tanks, educational organizations, networks, lobbying organizations, advocacy groups, organizations devoted to electoral politics, publishers, booksellers, and more.

The Advocates for Self-Government keeps up with this ever-growing movement and maintains an up-to-date list of the leading organizations — a gateway to the liberty movement.

Explore this list at www.Libertarianism.com.

188 · Libertarianism In One Lesson

ABOUT THE AUTHOR

David Bergland has a unique talent for explaining how libertarian principles apply to real-world problems. And he has spent a great deal of time doing just that — first as the Libertarian Party's vice presidential candidate in 1976 and as a candidate for U.S. Senate from California in 1980. He served as National Chairman of the Libertarian Party from 1977-1981 and again from 1998-2000.

Bergland was the Libertarian Party presidential candidate in 1984. He traveled throughout the country, learning the values and concerns of the American people. Much of what is in this book, and its earlier editions, is based on that experience.

Bergland holds a Bachelor's degree in English from the University of California at Los Angeles (UCLA) and a Juris Doctor degree from the University of Southern California (USC) School of Law. From 1970-1993, while in the private practice of law, he was also an Adjunct Professor of Law at Western State University College of Law in Fullerton, California and Irvine, California, where he taught Evidence, Civil Procedure, Property, Professional Responsibility, and Jurisprudence. Bergland is also a student of psychology and, in particular, its application to communication. He lectures and conducts workshops in this field.

Bergland has three daughters and seven grandchildren. He and his wife, Sharon Ayres, reside in Kennewick, Washington. Retired from the private practice of law, Bergland remains active as a writer, lecturer, and self-defense/martial arts instructor.

ABOUT THE ADVOCATES FOR SELF-GOVERNMENT

THE ADVOCATES FOR SELF-GOVERNMENT is a non-profit, non-partisan organization that encourages the public to understand and embrace libertarian ideas. To achieve that goal, the Advocates:

● Publicizes libertarian ideas to the public and to opinion leaders.

● Helps libertarians become more effective communicators of the ideas of liberty.

● Works to educate the public and opinion leaders about the true diversity of the world of politics. The old "left-vs.-right" model of the political spectrum is woefully inaccurate and misleading. A more accurate political "map" recognizes Liberal, Conservative, Centrist, Statist, and Libertarian viewpoints.

The Advocates for Self-Government offers numerous tools to achieve this mission. Premier among them is the World's Smallest Political Quiz, which measures people's political beliefs on a five-way chart. *The Washington Post* reported: "The Quiz has gained respect as a valid measure of a person's political leanings." The Quiz has been printed and publicized in political science textbooks, in newspapers and magazines, and on talk radio. Millions of people have taken the Quiz, and it is available online at www.TheAdvocates.org.

The Advocates publishes *The Liberator Online,* a free email newsletter that is the world's largest-circulation libertarian publication. The Advocates also publishes *The Libertarian Communicator,* a print magazine that teaches libertarians the best ways to take the message of liberty to the public.

The Advocates' Web site — www.TheAdvocates.org — has been widely acclaimed by top reviewers, including MSNBC, Yahoo!, and

Lycos, as one of the best political sites. This popular Web site features a comprehensive list of libertarian celebrities, links to libertarian radio talk show hosts, hundreds of articles, an online store, links to major libertarian organizations, and more. An affiliated site — www.Libertarianism.com — offers a beginner-friendly introduction to libertarianism.

Every year, the Advocates presents its Lights of Liberty Awards. The program encourages libertarians to take the ideas of liberty to the public — via letters to the editor, public speaking, and outreach booths. Since its launch in 1998, Lights of Liberty winners have taken libertarian ideas to millions of people.

The Advocates offers a wide array of communication and educational material, including books, tapes, and CDs. The Advocates also hosts regular seminars, workshops, and speeches, where Advocates representatives share the most effective communication methods with libertarian leaders and activists.

Leaders of the libertarian movement have been generous in their praise of the Advocates. U.S. Congressman Ron Paul (R-TX) said the Advocates has made "invaluable contributions to the freedom cause. I continue to be impressed by the Advocates' work." David Bergland, author of *Libertarianism in One Lesson*, said, "The Advocates is revolutionizing the libertarian movement." Political activist and actor Russell Means said, "Libertarians who want to get real should put into action what the Advocates teach." Mike Holmes of the Republican Liberty Caucus said, "The Advocates' teaching materials and instruction aids are the best I've seen in the movement."

The Advocates for Self-Government was founded in 1985 by Marshall Fritz. As a non-profit 501(c)(3) educational organization, contributions to the Advocates are tax-deductible. We welcome your support of our vital, world-changing work.

Contact the Advocates at: 269 Market Place Blvd. #106, Cartersville, GA 30121-2235. 800-932-1776. Fax: 770-386-8373. Email: info@TheAdvocates.org. Web site: www.TheAdvocates.org.